"IT WAS LIKE BEING IN THE CENTER OF A HURRICANE"
John Lennon

A TWIST OF LENNON explores the spectacular revolution in music and lifestyle begun and shaped by the Beatles—a revolution that influenced millions.

The rock 'n roll band which started so innocently in a Liverpool art college took control of the lives of the group and John's wife Cynthia, transporting them from obscurity to a world of limitless money, idolatry, and sumptuous living without precedent. Cynthia describes that unreal life—the personality changes, the conmen and hangers-on, the groupies, the drugs, the jet-setters, and finally the appearance of Yoko Ono. Beyond that, Cynthia Lennon captures the magic of the Beatles, a magic that will not die!

WITH PERSONAL PHOTOGRAPHS AND THE AUTHOR'S ORIGINAL DRAWINGS

A Twist of

Lennon

By Cynthia Lennon

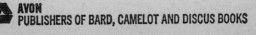
AVON
PUBLISHERS OF BARD, CAMELOT AND DISCUS BOOKS

AVON BOOKS
A division of
The Hearst Corporation
959 Eighth Avenue
New York, New York 10019

First Avon Printing, January, 1980
Second Printing

AVON TRADEMARK REG. U.S. PAT. OFF. AND IN
OTHER COUNTRIES, MARCA REGISTRADA,
HECHO EN U.S.A.

Printed in the U.S.A.

Contents

1

War Baby

You may remember a famous comedian whose act began: 'The day war broke out, my missus said to me . . .' Well, the day war broke out my mother was expecting her third and *positively* last child—me! But with His Majesty's Government's emergency evacuation measures coinciding with this promised addition to the family (my mother thinking she had long ago looked the last dirty nappy in the face) there was very little to laugh about.

For my two brothers, Tony and Charles, evacuation meant being transported lock, stock and bottle of pop from a densely populated part of Liverpool to the nether regions of North Wales. It could have been outer Mongolia as far as they were concerned. But by all accounts they fared better with their adopted family than my mother, who, like hundreds of other pregnant mums at that time, was carted off to Blackpool, Lancs.

Just picture the scene. Autumn 1939. Grey days in every respect. The place, Blackpool-by-the-sea. Dozens of that now infamous breed of seaside landladies waiting expectantly behind multi-coloured curtains and well-watered aspidistras. Equally expectantly, numerous hotel managers busily made rooms available for their even more expectant guests. Finally and in their coachloads, pregnant mums of all shapes, sizes and creeds began their own private invasion.

Separated from their families at a time of national and personal crisis, emotions were running high and it was a bedraggled bewildered tearful little band of comrades-in-arms which surrounded my mother on the doorstep of her allotted Holiday Hotel. They were duly escorted inside their temporary home by a local Government official and introduced to their particular fate—the landlady. As it happened she was only too pleased to relieve the Government of its money for providing lodgings, but found it too irksome to actually provide beds!

My mother's happy event was due to take place in three days time, but the conditions were appalling. Food was rationed to a minimum despite the fact that it was only the first week of the war. On account of that, the lack of welcome and warmth, and the landlady's ultimatum that it was 'Two to a single bed', war really broke out! Bewildered as they were, their Liverpudlian tempers were raised. Aware of their rights, the visiting aliens insisted on leaving to find accommodation suitable to their condition. Once more the motley crew set out into the unknown, now minus the official in charge.

Lost in this strange part of the country, this troupe of intrepid worn-out mothers began their search in what seemed a world gone mad. The entire population of Blackpool consisted of servicemen, landladies, expectant mothers and crying toddlers (too young to be separated from their mothers by any emergency measures). Finding a 'room-with-a-view' was no easy task, but their prayers were answered when from the entrance of a rather splendid hotel a young man hailed the weary travellers and kindly ushered them into the foyer and from there into the dining room, where tables were laid with food and drink for all. The young man explained that his quota of ladies had not arrived so the welcome mat was out for my mother and her group for the first time since they had left their homes that morning. Fed and watered they were put to bed.

The following day, after a restless night in a strange bed, my mother went into the first stages of labour and was immediately transferred to the 'House of Temporary Labour', yet another hostelry of ill repute! She was installed in a room of minute proportions and equally minute facilities, comprising of a bed, a bucket and a brass

'The day war broke out my missus said to me'

bed head to hang on to. That was it. She was then left to her own devices for a day and a night. The following day a midwife entered the cell realizing it was about time something was done for my mother if I was to be born into this world. She was a good woman and knew at once that if she didn't do something drastic mother and I were not going to make it. To add to the chaos she was without instruments of any description for assisting with problem births. The conditions were dreadful.

On that wet miserable Sunday, September 10th, 1939, my Father arrived by train from Liverpool knowing nothing of my mother's ordeal. But taking one look at her, he burst into tears and was promptly sent out for a walk in the rain, with the promise of a child within the hour. That promise was kept. The door to that grimy, claustrophobic room was locked, my mother was sworn to secrecy for what was about to take place, and I was literally dragged into this beautiful world by the hair, ears, nose—anything she could get hold of. That midwife went against all the rules in the medical book but I thank her for it now. She saved my life and my mother's sanity.

Our hurried exodus followed. As soon as my mother was strong enough to travel she refused emphatically to stay, packed her bags and left against all medical advice. As it happened she need never have left Liverpool in the first place. No bombs, no catastrophes, nothing untoward had happened in our absence. But she was a great deal wiser after her ordeal and thanked God I was alive and kicking.

That school days are the happiest days is a question of personal experience, and in many cases the luck of the draw. But in my case all my dreams were, despite a shaky start, fulfilled at the age of twelve.

I had always been a very timid child—'Very conscientious, but lacks confidence', was the gist of my school reports and this judgement was firmly imprinted on my mind from a very early age. But in one subject, Art, I shone.

Following my failure to pass the Eleven Plus, I went to the local secondary school, a failure in my own eyes mainly because all my close friends were successful. Needless to say I cultivated painting and drawing and was rewarded on a number of occasions by the Liverpool Echo printing my work on the Children's Page. Oh, the thrill of it all . . . Fame and Fortune . . . Local girl makes good . . . My fortune amounted to a pound, a small fortune indeed to a little girl in those days. But it wasn't the money that thrilled me, it was the realization that I had a recognizable talent for something. I was offered the opportunity soon to sit an examination for entrance into the Liverpool Junior Art School. I couldn't believe it, I was at last being given a chance to prove myself in a subject I adored, a subject I understood. I passed, and for the first time I could see my future opening up before me. The sheer delight I experienced at the thought of travelling daily to Liverpool by train, a train journey with businessmen and women as my companions. I suddenly felt a woman of the world even though I was still wearing ankle socks and school uniform. An added bonus to my passing the exam was the fact that at the age of eighteen, I would have the opportunity to enter the College of Art proper. Liverpool was a City of Character and wonderful characters, and I was to be part of it.

The Junior Art School was all it promised to be. The teachers were marvellous, their enthusiasm was boundless and as a result the pupils were very keen, competitive, and above all happy. The sheer quality of work produced at the school during those years was tremendous. I received a wonderful preparation for what I presumed would be eventual acceptance at the Seminar College. But, when I was seventeen my beloved father died of cancer following a six-month illness. My mother had known three months before his death that there was no way that he would recover. All the time I was carrying on with my studies for the General Certificate of Education examinations, my Father was dying very painfully. He was wasting away in front of our eyes, but despite the drugs he was aware that something dreadful was happening to him and his main concern was that as soon as I had finished junior school I should get a job of work and earn some money. He reasoned that we were going to need every penny we could lay our hands on.

Certainly I knew my father was very ill, but I didn't

know that he was dying. The dreams that I had cherished of going to College were suddenly shattered. I couldn't understand at that time why or how life could be so cruel. Children can be very selfish when they don't understand, and I was no exception!

The sad loss of my father in June 1956 weighed very heavily on the whole family but we carried on as people must under such tragic circumstances. I continued with my studies, got myself a steady boyfriend and eventually passed the 'O' levels and 'A' level that I had taken in GCE. My mother then came to my rescue as far as my future education was concerned. On my father's death my mother had received a certain amount of insurance money, and it was she who gave me hope again by saying 'You go to College love, we'll manage.' She knew how much it meant to me and she went out of her way to help. It was in the Autumn of 1957 that I began my studies at the Liverpool College of Art. I was just eighteen.

The sense of freedom and independence I felt in my first term at college was exhilarating and was summed up by the change from school uniform to the arty gear of the student, all drawing boards and duffle coats. It was, at last, a uniform of choice. We all felt that we must look the part, as bohemian as possible. I revelled in the whole Art School image, but of course it was some time before my integration into the new way of life was complete.

At the beginning when asked by my fellow students where I came from, I would reply, 'I come from Hoylake, on the Wirral.' Scousers (inhabitants of Liverpool) would look at me as if I was something the cat had dragged in and reply. 'Oh! (long pause) You come from over the water (the river Mersey) do you?' They would then proceed to pass the time of day with someone they thought they could communicate with more easily, namely another scouser. It has always been the same with Liverpudlians. They believe that if you live over the water you think you are better than they. You either own a pony or you have two or three cars, one for yourself and one for each foot. As it happened in our particular case the family 'mansion' was a terraced house in a seaside village and the nearest thing we had to a garage was the coal-shed.

The trouble was that those of us unlucky enough to live over the water spoke 'different', and that difference to the scouser meant 'posh' and I'm afraid that didn't go down very well in Liverpool. No airs and graces are permitted if you want to be accepted, and I did.

I began my college education with my over-the-water image, twin-set and tweed skirt, short permed hair and worst of all glasses. Can you imagine the swinging impression I made? It was non-existent. Oh yes, and a name like Cynthia. A name given to all the snooty school prefects in the popular girls' magazines of the time . . . disaster. I was and still am a very shy person which made matters still worse. My self-consciousness and lack of sparkling conversation gave everyone the false impression of aloofness. If only they had known the agonies I was going through at the time. Anyway I put up with it all and took everything in. At the same time I threw myself into my beloved art which after all was why I was there. And I had my close friend Phyllis for company. Phyl came from the Junior Art School with me so our friendship was long lasting. We were both very conscientious; we were there to work, and we were not amused by that rowdy lot.

The first two years at college were spent studying the many and varied techniques of art. We took courses in Pottery, Silversmithing, Architecture and Lettering, to name but a few. At the end of the two year course it was hoped we would have a good idea of what subject we were going to specialise in for our National Diploma. But first we had to choose a subject to specialise in for our intermediate exam. My choice was Lettering. My emotional life at this time was centred around a local chap. He was my first serious love and as far as I was concerned, this was *it*. He was even saving up each week in the Building Society for our future, so life really seemed mapped out for me at that stage, and I was very happy at the prospect. Little did I know what was around the corner.

As far as I can remember Lettering took place twice a week and about a dozen of us had opted for it through choice, but there was one amongst us who didn't seem to fit into our neat little band of letterers, his name was John Winston Lennon.

The reason he didn't seem to fit was that he had had no choice to which course he took . . . *nobody* wanted him. John's particular talents hadn't gone unnoticed but they weren't his artistic talents. They were his talents for having his fellow students fall about with shocked, uncontrollable laughter at his wicked, disrespectful wit. His ability to disrupt a lecture had to be seen to be believed and John's appearance was even worse than his humour. I think he was the last stronghold of the Teddy Boys— totally aggressive and anti-establishment. My first impression of John, as he slouched reluctantly into the lettering class for the first time, was one of apprehension. I felt that I had nothing in common with this individual and as far as I was concerned I never would. In fact he frightened me to death. The only thing that John and I had in common was that we were both blind as bats without our glasses.

Nevertheless, from the moment John Winston Lennon made his presence felt in my naïve little world, my life began to turn upside down. He spent the rest of the week in College in a different group to me so I only came into contact with him on lettering days. He would usually arrive late, sit behind me and spend the whole day borrowing my precious equipment (for being a conscientious student I always had the right equipment for the job in hand). The trouble was that every week I would arrive home minus a ruler or a favourite paint brush. This persistent state of affairs did not enhance my views of this uncouth character, who had invaded my well-ordered life.

Well ordered that is at college for on the emotional front things began to disintegrate. My love life was in ruins; my steady boy-friend had eyes for another. I just couldn't believe it . . . the end of the world for me. He lived very near to me but the competition lived even nearer. The pain and humiliation of it all was unbearable. My part as the tragic Queen lasted six months by which time after countless walks with my dog in the vicinity of his home at all times of the day and night I got the message and gave up.

Following a carefree and unattached period at college (including one or two lovely innocent relationships with

14

students I knew) my first love returned. 'Couldn't live without you, I didn't realize how much you meant to me,' etc., etc. As it happened I still cared a great deal for him and succumbed. Once more I was attached and to begin with happier for it. But for all my regained equilibrium something was not quite right. Suddenly lettering days were becoming increasingly important to me. The John Lennon I had so readily avoided on first meeting was beginning to get under my skin, he was becoming a source of fascination to me. A larger than life character, a rebel. Hilariously funny in a dry sick way, but totally fascinating. John's drawings and cartoons were repulsively funny. I found myself more and more wanting to find out what made him tick. This of course was all against my better judgement, but I was unable to do anything about it.

My feelings for John came to a head in a very strange way. In fact they erupted one day in the lecture theatre . . . On this particular day all the intermediate students were gathered together for a discussion. We all straggled in as usual, motley crew as we were. Amidst the chaos I noted that I was sitting directly behind John and his bunch of camp followers. When the lecture began it was interrupted as usual by a few scattered Lennonisms followed by stifled shrieks and giggles. I was really enjoying the performance until a friend of mine who was sitting next to John jokingly started stroking his hair and my God, I was consumed with jealousy! I couldn't believe it. From that moment I was totally infatuated. Quite honestly my emotions had never been put to such a test before and I was confused.

During the following weeks I couldn't get the image of John out of my mind. It puzzled me constantly how and why I could be attracted so strongly to him. He just wasn't my idea of the ideal boy-friend in any way. In fact the thought of it frightened me to death. Of course I was jumping the gun. I don't think he was even aware of my existence at that point, except of course as a soft touch for artists' materials or someone to poke fun at now and again. He lived in a different world to me.

Lettering days became my fix. It was the only time I had any close contact with John. I would arrive before

15

anyone else so that I could sit near to where he had been sitting the previous week. To do what? I really didn't know. I was always backward in coming forward. I just had to study this object of my obsession at close quarters. John would frequently breeze into the class battered guitar slung over one shoulder, black drainpipe trousers, hair meticulously greased back, his side-burns grown as long as he could possibly grow them. The expression on John's face was always one of challenge and it went with his image. The hard knock. The angry young man.

John's real love, of course, was music. On one or two occasions I watched him perch awkwardly on top of a desk and quietly play and sing, transporting himself from the abhorrent world of lettering to his dream world. It was then that I noticed a totally different expression on John's face. It softened. All the aggression lifted. At last there was something I had seen in John that I could understand.

After integrating myself into college life, I decided it was time I made the most of myself. At the very least I would look as if I belonged, so I started growing my hair. It was a rather nondescript colour, but I had convinced myself that when the sun shone on it, it had beautiful golden tints, at least that is what my mother had always told me.

So now I was going 'au naturel'. My wardrobe was the second point of attack. Off with the old and on with the black velvet trousers and duffle coat. Great! Then, finally, my attention moved to the dreaded glasses. My decision never to wear them again spelt disaster. My work became . . . well, let's say (to be polite) 'impressionistic'. And my daily bus ride from Liverpool Central to the College led me more times than I cared to remember far from my destination into the suburbs of Liverpool. On the positive side, though, I did become a competent lip-reader and the individual sounds of my friends' footsteps had a recognizable ring to them. In fact all my other faculties were worked to death. At last I gave in and struck a highly intellectual bespectacled figure at work, the rest of the time whipping them on and off.

16

The strange thing about all this preoccupation with glasses was that it was a discussion about glasses that brought me to the attention of John. My fellow students were testing each other's eyesight one morning only to discover that John and I had almost identical lack of vision. This earth shattering discovery brought us to a new high point of communication. It was the only time in my life that I was thankful for my disability and our recollections on the subject of near blindness were hilarious. Anyway, I thought so at the time, and we had broken the ice at last.

The ice had been broken but neither of us was ready to take the plunge. The pain of it all got worse. My concentration was going. My every movement was geared to —'Will he, won't he be there. What will I do or say if he is?' It was awful, I just couldn't see a way out.

My mother was sure I must have been sickening for something. My eating habits changed dramatically—fading away I was. I would leave for College earlier, come home later. The excuses I conjured up were awe inspiring to say the least. 'Well, Mum I am needed early in the morning to help set up equipment . . . and in the evening I am doing extra mural studies.' In fact I was spending miserable, agonizing hours wandering the draughty College corridors just in the hope of a glimpse. Phyllis thought I was mad. I was of course, but underlying all this out-of-character behaviour was the real thrill of being in love with someone who was to my mind unobtainable. It was like living on the edge of a precipice, and it was very exciting. I enjoyed every minute of it in a weird sort of way.

All this love-sick mooning and time-wasting was taking place during my second year at College, but as it so happened I had not gone completely unnoticed by the object of my attentions. It was coming up to the Summer vacation and we were all in a true holiday spirit. So much so that one of the students thought it would be a great idea to have a bit of a 'do' one lunchtime, before breaking up. Everyone agreed any excuse was as good as none. So it was arranged. Permission was granted for us to use the smallest room in the College. It didn't matter what size

17

it was, we were all set to go. Someone supplied a record player plus the latest discs. A contribution was made by all for the booze and the date was set.

I must admit I was really looking forward to this party. I thought it would take my mind off John Lennon for a while. I was sure that he wouldn't be having anything to do with a tame students' get-together. He just didn't seem the type. Phyl and I thought it would make a change and provide a giggle or two to finish off the term. Well it did provide me with a giggle of sorts. In fact I nearly died laughing. He was there! I couldn't stand it. My legs turned to jelly, my face was the colour of an over-ripe Victoria plum; and there just wasn't a corner to hide in. What I had dreamed of for so long had become a nightmare. I just couldn't cope with the situation at such close quarters and was convinced that everyone in that room could see what was written all over my face.

Of course no one was the least bit interested in my emotional state. All they wanted was to enjoy themselves and to make the most of the lunchtime session while they could. I was finally able to regain my composure and join in the fun and chat relaxing more and more by the drinkful. I was not then an experienced drinker, so the effect was immediate. The sun was shining, the music was great and what I wanted to happen most happened. John asked me to dance, and I nearly died. Bingo! I then amazed myself by being very cool, calm and collected outwardly—inside I was out of this world. The dance was slow and smoochy. I was aloof and John, I think, was slightly embarrassed. It was all very painful and beautiful at the same time. The remaining students were looking on with puzzled expressions at such an unlikely combination.

The party began to break up. It was time to get back to the drawing board, but John drew me aside, questioning me about my availability. I was so nonplussed by the question that my reply came back quickly.

'I'm awfully sorry, I'm engaged to this fellow in Hoylake.'

John's face dropped a mile, but not to be out-done his answer to that was, 'I didn't ask you to marry me did I?'

18

I blew it, at least that's what I thought. I'd thrown my chance out of the window. But not so, John and his mates then proceeded to invite Phyl and I out for a drink to the local boozer. Even though everything seemed to be going well I was really terrified of what I was letting myself in for. I had a feeling of impending doom about the whole situation. Where on earth would we go from here?

In fact I was so besotted with John that I decided there and then to let fate take over. I would just go with the tide and hope that I landed on the shore in one piece.

As it happened the pub was bursting at the seams. Everyone had had the same idea. Anyone with any curiosity must have been well aware that there was something blooming between that madman Lennon and that . . . what's her name?—twin-set Cynthia from over the water. The whole situation was very embarrassing. I was tongue-tied. Phyl and I giggled a great deal on finding ourselves out of our usual environment surrounded by heaving, boozing bodies. No one could move and you couldn't hear yourself speak, but it was marvellous. So this was what everyone did at lunchtime. We began to realize just what we had been missing. All work and no play had really made us dull girls.

After being bought, and having bought ourselves, quite a few drinks I was becoming slightly tipsy, especially as I had eaten nothing since early morning. John was huddled together with his crowd of admirers, and I was beginning to feel as though I had been set up as some sort of joke. My heart sank. The joke really was on me if that were true, so I thought it would be wise to take our leave as discreetly as possible. But before we could get out the loud voice of Lennon saying, 'Didn't you know Miss Powell (my name at the time) was a nun then?' rose above the noise of the pub. I was dragged back into focus and persuaded to stay. How could I resist?

That folks is how an incredible chapter in my life began, a most unlikely beginning to what became a veritable shooting star. A star that landed me back to earth with one hell of a bump only eight years later. But what a lifetime in eight years.

To My Father

My Father's love is ever present,
The thoughts of him forever pleasant,
My love for him undying,
At all times I find I'm trying
To continue in his goodness,
Carry on his works of kindness,
Ever conscious of his spirit,
Ever willing to inherit,
All his qualities remembered.

To descend from such a man
What thanks I offer for this plan.
Perhaps he will never know how
        much.
I miss his understanding—human bliss.
The precious times we spent together,
His moment of death just couldn't
        sever
The bond between his love and mine.
He lives within my heart and time.

2

Growing Up With the Beatles

Following that auspicious party John and I saw as much of each other as was humanly possible. John was living at that time with his Aunt Mimi in Woolton a rather posh suburb of Liverpool. From my earlier description of John you wouldn't have thought it possible, but many aspects of John's life amazed me as our relationship grew. We spent that long summer holiday, meeting, eating and sleeping together as often as we could. The expense of travelling to Liverpool frequently proved to be a great strain on the purse and my long-suffering mother was losing patience with her errant daughter.

At about this time John had become very friendly with a fellow student called Stuart. Stuart was an exceptionally sensitive young man. He was a marvellous artist, one of the outstanding students of the time. I think Stuart was as fascinated as I with the character of John Lennon and very soon he came under his influence as most of John's friends did. It was to Stuart's flat, or should I say bedsit, that John and I escaped following the drinking session at the pub on the day that we finally came out in the open with each other. There was no question in my mind about whether or not we should make love. It happened so naturally. Nothing else mattered to either of us at the time. We wanted to get as close to each other as was humanly possible. From that moment our commitment to each other was total. Although John and I were as seriously involved as any two young people could be, neither of us had any idea where our relationship would lead. Our thoughts were of today not tomorrow. Tomorrow didn't exist as far as we were concerned. My past, present and future, were totally absorbed in the mood of the moment, in the mood of the man I loved. And John was a moody man.

John had had a very tragic upbringing, his mother and father having separated while he was still a young child. By all accounts John's mum, Julia, was a fantastic character with a marvellous sense of humour not unlike her son's. Most important, as it turned out, she was musical. John's father, Freddy, was a seafaring man and the long separations did little to help a marriage which had begun so beautifully. Eventually Freddy failed to come home at all and Julia was left to fend for herself. Young, attractive and talented, Julia felt the need to lead her own life and in the knowledge that John's Aunt Mimi would provide a secure and happy home life it was decided that Mimi should bring him up.

Mimi had her work well and truly cut out for although it was not until he was in his teens that John began to form an ever-increasing chip on his shoulder, his total lack of respect towards authority of any kind created havoc at school. He was at war with the world and everyone in it. The school staff despaired of him and to them it appeared as if the only enjoyment he gained from life was at the expense of the weak in and out of authority. Mimi's numerous visits to the school to keep things on an even keel paid off, however, and the frequent threats of expulsion for John's outrageous behaviour thankfully came to naught.

Obvious as it was to all that John would never be eligible for the Brain of Britain, a very understanding teacher recognized John's natural intelligence and creative abilities and it was he who pointed John in the direction of the Liverpool College of Art. When John was accepted there, following an interview at which he wore Uncle George's suit, shirt and tie (Mimi's husband had died suddenly of a heart attack years before), it was a heartfelt relief to his aunt.

During his teens John saw more and more of Julia and they became very close. She taught him to play the guitar;

22

she herself played the banjo and sang. John must have been elated to find her more of a friend to him than a mother—someone he could communicate with so easily on all levels. John once told me that his mother would go for a walk with him wearing a pair of knickers on her head as a hat and a pair of old glasses without lenses. She would then stop to ask someone the way and start scratching her eye through the lense-less glasses, the expression on her face remaining completely dead-pan whilst doing so. Their sense of humour was almost identical and John must have been on top of the world at that time. However, life was to be very cruel to them both. Their happiness came to an abrupt and tragic end. Julia, following a visit to John and Mimi, left to catch a late bus home. The bus stop was a mere two hundred yards away, across a busy main road, but Julia didn't make it. As she was crossing the road she was knocked down by a hit-and-run driver and died almost immediately. John was left full of emptiness and bitterness, and the hard exterior he built was self-protective. He didn't want to be hurt any more. It was in music that he could best express himself, music and art.

Once back at college after our summer break John and I were inseparable. John's friends at the time were few, but very close. I was in for a very testing time with them. In the beginning I think I was a bit of a joke to them; I just wasn't John's type. No way could they see it lasting. 'She's from over the water; she doesn't look anything like Brigitte.' (Bardot was John's dream girl.) 'She's not funny; what on earth does he see in her? It can't be for real . . .' Nothing was said but I knew by their faces and reactions what was going on in their heads. For my part I was sure I would never be accepted and John too was up against a great deal of criticism from my friends. 'You must be out of your mind; he's a nut-case; you'll get nothing but trouble from that one; you're really asking for it aren't you?' There was opposition from all sides. But no one was going to interfere with our love, no matter how much truth there was in their arguments. We loved each other and that was all that mattered to us.

John and I used to have our lunch at the back of the

stage in the canteen so that we could have some privacy. And it was there that we were frequently joined by two friends of John from the school next door to the college— George and Paul. Their school uniforms hung uncomfortably on their rather thin gangly frames. Paul was an old friend of John; George a comparatively new one. I remember they were both so keen and enthusiastic, not about school, but music: guitars and the latest Chuck Berry, Bo Diddley and Buddy Holly. Paul played the guitar and George was learning frantically. They would bring in their fish and chips and their enthusiasm, and talk for as long as time allowed. At first I felt very much an outsider. I had never heard of half of the people they were ranting on about. If they had been talking about Frank Sinatra, fine, or even Tchaikovsky, great, but who the heck was Bo Diddley? I didn't have the foggiest, but I was soon to be given a crash course in rock and roll and also to learn how two students could survive on eight shillings a day. My travelling expenses came to two shillings. And John was always broke. Guitar strings were expensive and cigarettes made quite a hole in a student's allowance— and that was before the pub visits at lunchtime. Times were very hard, but great fun.

On one occasion, a crowd of us went for a lunchtime drink to our local, The Crack. We were all having a laugh and a black velvet, when we sensed there was some excitement going on outside the pub. We rushed out to see what was up only to be confronted by a beautiful shiny sports car and the easily recognizable face and figure of John Gregson, actual star of stage, screen and *Genevieve*. You could have knocked me down with a feather, but not John. He rushed off out of sight and returned carrying a dirty old boot in his hands and eagerly presented it to John Gregson saying, 'Can I have your autograph please, guv.' John was obviously thrilled to bits with his find, he wouldn't have dreamed of asking for an autograph with something so commonplace as a piece of paper but a boot, well you can't beat that for something out of the ordinary. John Gregson was highly amused. He signed on the dotted stitching and drove off into the sunset. A lovely little incident to look back on.

John and I would go to the pictures as often as we could, when we had enough money between us. We loved watching films, but the added bonus of being able to be close and warm together, for a few hours at least, was bliss. If we couldn't afford the luxury of the cinema we would visit the local Chinese coffee bar, where we became famous for making a cup of coffee last as long as two hours at a sitting. The proprietors seemed to understand the plight of the penniless student and John and I in those early days would just sit opposite each other, hold each other's hands under the formica table, and gaze avidly into each other's moon-struck eyes. The place could have collapsed about our ears for all the notice we were taking of the world about us. John would tell me a lot about himself on occasions such as these. My curiosity was insatiable. I wanted to know what made him tick; why he dressed like a down and out Teddy boy when his home and background were decidedly middle class.

John would explain that if you looked hard then there was more chance of survival when you came across a gang of tough guys. If you looked like them they were less likely to batter you than if you were dressed in arty gear and glasses. John was a self-confessed coward, but if he was really pushed he could fight as dirty as his attackers and frequently did in the old days. On the other hand, he would use every trick in the book to avoid a confrontation. If you'd ever come across a bunch of roughnecks in Liverpool, you'd find it easy enough to understand John's strategy—it was a case of the survival of the fittest.

I realized early on in our relationship that life with John was not going to be all hearts and roses. His insecurity had created an angry young man persona and I had to be prepared to take the full impact of his unreasonable rages. Everything would appear to be happiness and contentment one moment, and the next moment all hell would break loose. I would be accused of not loving enough, of being unfaithful, of looking or talking to a member of the opposite sex for too long. John's jealousy and possessiveness were at times unbearable and I found myself a quaking, nervous wreck on many an occasion—so much so that the thought of going into college the following day would

25

fill me with fear and dread. I just had no idea what was in store for me. It was such a strange love I had for John I was totally under his spell but I was really quite terrified of him for seventy-five per cent of the time. He tested me to the limits of my endurance. The one thought that kept me going during that time was that if I could last it out, John's faith in human nature would be restored. If he could believe in just one person, he would be well on the way to calming his troubled spirit, and I desperately wanted to see him at peace with himself and the world, for his sake and mine.

Although I had many opportunities to disentangle myself from John, I just couldn't make the break. I was faithful to him at all times. When I wasn't seeing him, I would be at home with my mother watching television, or doing college work until the early hours of the morning. My social life revolved around John and John alone. When I was out with him he would make sure that I didn't leave until the last train to Hoylake came in. I would then scramble into a carriage full of drunks and late night jokers. I was more often than not the only female on the train at that late hour, all the rest had more sense than me. It was a nightmare journey. I would find a corner seat, get out a large newspaper or a book and hide behind it, making myself as inconspicuous as was humanly possible. I wish I had been the type who could make light of a situation like that and laugh it off, but being me, painfully self-conscious, I just died with embarrassment and nerves. Those twenty minutes always seemed the longest of my life.

George and Paul often came into the college canteen in those days. George was the tender age of sixteen, Paul seventeen, John eighteen and I was nineteen. Babies really. Paul did his best to look like a student. He would wear a mac or overcoat buttoned up to the neck in order to hide the school uniform that he disliked so intensely. His hair was as long as school rules would permit and his big soulful eyes would gaze around the canteen with envy, looking forward in desperation to the day when he could leave school and blaze his own trail.

As the college term was coming to an end and examinations were imminent, we seemed to have whole days with very little to do, the theory being that if we weren't competent after two years of work then we never would be. Consequently we were given a great deal of time off to relax before the dreaded intermediate exams. It was on such days as these that John and I would leave the college portals hand in hand for an afternoon at the cinema or a bus ride to see Aunt Mimi in Woolton, just happy being in each other's company for a while. It wouldn't be for long, though. Wandering along lost to the world we would be brought down to earth with a bump by a piercing whistle or yell from behind us that could only mean one thing—George.

'Hi John, Hi Cyn.' He would hurriedly catch us up and then it would be, 'Where are you two off to? Can I come?' Neither of us would have the heart to tell this thin gangly kid in school uniform to push off. Poor George! He hadn't really got to the stage of serious girlfriends yet and was totally unaware of what it was all about, Alfie! So we would spend the lost afternoon as a jolly threesome, wondering what on earth we were going to do with ourselves.

On other occasions when Paul just 'happened' to be off school too, we would take a bus, and the guitars, to the home where a friend of John's mother lived. Twitchy was the irreverent nickname John had bestowed upon him. Twitchy was a head waiter and worked odd hours. John had worked it all out that the house would be empty. The whole situation seemed very wrong to me. 'How on earth do we get in?' I asked, full of apprehension. John's reply didn't put my mind at rest at all. 'Oh, don't worry about a simple thing like that, he usually leaves his larder window open.' The window was slightly open and proved to be large enough for one of the errant band to squeeze through. Once in, the front door would be opened and the rush to get in broke all records. Once ensconced, illegally or otherwise, the boys would sit cross-legged on the floor, tune up their guitars and begin practising. The music would delight me, the worry and fear of what would happen if we were interrupted disappeared and I would be caught up in the harmony and joy of the music I was listening to. John, Paul and George were totally absorbed in their music. They would listen intently to their records, and then make dedicated attempts at reproducing the sound. I was really becoming hooked on the music that they made, unpolished as it was in those early days.

The session usually lasted about two hours. During this time the larder would be duly raided and tea made. Cheese butties, or anything else for that matter, would be downed, the house would be left as we had found it and we would be away before you could say Bo Diddley. It was following one such occasion that George confided in John his thoughts about my suitability as a girl-friend. 'I think she's great, John, but there is one thing wrong.' Long pause . . . 'What's that, George?' John asked. George replied with a certain amount of trepidation, 'Well, it's her teeth, she's got teeth like a horse.'

The intermediate exams were upon us before any of us had time to think a great deal about them. The atmosphere in college was serious, the carefree attitudes of the students changed dramatically to mild hysteria and near panic. Here was the crunch. Fail the exam and we would be out on our ears, with no qualifications to assist us in the big bad world. We all seemed to age over night at the unsavoury prospects of that dirty word *failure*. The usual misgivings abounded. If only we hadn't spent so much time in that bloody pub; if only we hadn't taken so much time off when we could have been working; if only . . . Oh well, it was too late to worry, we just had to do our best, such as it was.

Once the exams were over we were *free*, the weight and the worry were lifted, our futures were in the lap of the gods so we set about the happy task of enjoying ourselves once more. The summer vacation was upon us and results of our examinations wouldn't be forthcoming until late in August, so we could relax for a while. A great deal of commuting between Hoylake and Liverpool was done during the holidays and John and I spent a lot of our time with Stuart Sutcliffe. Stuart shared a flat in a very large house in Gambia Terrace, very close to college and almost next door to my beloved Junior Art School.

Stuart's part of the flat consisted of one enormous room, totally devoid of any home comforts. A double mattress

28

lay desolately in one corner of the room underneath a large, dirty window, bare of anything remotely resembling a curtain. The floor-boards were spotted with different coloured oil paint; an easel was in evidence which seemed to dominate the room; canvasses finished or abandoned in a fit of artistic frustration were scattered around without semblance of order. Stuart's flat was the archetype of a poverty-stricken artist's studio. My first impression of this flat was one of horror. How could he live in such conditions? Chip papers filled the sooty fireplace; tubes of half-used oil paint were piled up on the mantelpiece; the walls were adorned with posters and beautiful charcoal sketches of the nude figure of the college's life model, June. I wanted desperately to get to work on the flat for him. The mothering instinct came on very strong. Stuart always looked as though he needed someone to love and care for him. He was a very slight figure, his whole demeanor was one of sensitivity and gentleness. Art to Stuart was his whole life, comfort and home luxuries were of little importance to him and as long as he had somewhere to lay his head at night and enough money to buy paints and canvasses, he was happy. His room was his castle and his independence and freedom to work on his art surmounted every other need.

On one particular visit to Stuart it emerged that he would love to be involved in music. The influence John had over Stuart was very strong and the urge to communicate with John on every level was important to him at that time. John came up with a suggestion that seemed to suit everyone. George at the time played lead guitar, Paul and John concentrated on rhythm guitar so they were really in need of a bass player in the group. Stuart, with all his enthusiasm, could possibly fill that space. But it would mean starting from scratch and learning quickly.

He was over the moon when John came up with this suggestion. The main drawback, of course, was the absence of a bass guitar. The mere thought of the price of the instrument was daunting to say the least to a student on a very limited government grant but Stuart was not to be put off by such trifles. He scraped enough money together to put a down payment on a new bass guitar and put himself very much in debt to acquire the instrument. But that was of little importance to him, he had what he wanted and was determined to make full use of it.

If anyone deserved success in whatever they did it was Stuart. With John's help he mastered the basic guitar chords in next to no time. Every spare moment was taken up practising, struggling to better his speed and technique, hoping for words of praise from John for his efforts, which John gave when they were really warranted. The particular problems Stuart had to contend with were coping with the size of the bass (Stuart was only tiny and the guitar was quite large to handle) and his poor blistered, bleeding fingers. The hardening of the skin on the fingers is normally a slow process but with Stuart he wanted to be able to play proficiently, yesterday! Consequently his fingers were in a terrible state as the taut strings cut painfully and relentlessly into his skin.

With the end of the summer holidays came our examination results. Gloom pervaded: I passed with flying colours but John's results were a different matter altogether. He had failed in the subject he loathed most, Lettering. What now? The matter was in the hands of the head of the college and the education authorities. We could only keep our fingers crossed. As it happened luck was on our side. John was to be given the opportunity of taking the Lettering exam again the following year but in the meantime he was to carry on working for the National Diploma in Design. The Diploma course, lasting two years, involved specialization in a particular subject, only partly of one's own choice.

Although I have said Stuart was influenced by John, John was also influenced by Stuart in different ways. He was in awe of Stuart's paintings and they inspired John to enter the painting department for the following two years. I, on the other hand, plumped for illustration, a subject which appealed to me and was clearly suited to my particular talents.

Now John, as I found out with time, was very attractive to the opposite sex. He held a great fascination for girls and the thought of being in separate departments didn't exactly fill me with joy. But our relationship was relatively

'Oh no John no John no!'

young and our feelings for each other were very strong, so I really didn't think there was much danger of losing him to anybody at that time.

The Autumn term commenced with great excitement. The new courses were a challenge, and the fact that we were one step further up the ladder of our careers made us feel older and more confident for the future. We weren't the babies of the college any more. John and I spent whatever free time we had with each other, but our ups and downs, jealousies and petty rows continued interspersed with times of love and happiness. John's unpredictable urge to lash out verbally and physically continued, especially when he had a few drinks. The hurt was very deeply engraved inside him, but his irrepressible humour was always very much in evidence. For example, on our way to Mimi's we would sit upstairs on the bus, usually on the back seat because John couldn't do without his ciggies. On one occasion, sitting innocently directly in front of us, was a bald-headed chap on his way home from a hard day's work, the Liverpool *Echo* perched in front of him, dreaming, no doubt, of the lamb scouse he was expecting for his dinner. John, without changing his expression, proceeded to tickle his bald patch very gently, hurriedly snatching his hand away just as the poor unsuspecting man went to scratch the annoying itch. This carried on until the man's face grew redder and redder. His peace totally destroyed and his evening paper on the floor, he was reduced to a nervous wreck and still totally unsuspecting. The culprit remained unmoved, his face revealing nothing, even when the poor man looked around in the vain hope of discovering what was causing his embarrassing discomfort. John gazed out of the window and started whistling as though he was completely unaware of anything except the view. For my own part the embarrassment couldn't be contained. I went all colours of the rainbow, sweating profusely. All my sympathy went out to the victim. When finally we alighted from the bus I breathed a sigh of relief, but it was premature. Once off the bus John began stage two of his performance, to make sure that everyone on the bus was on the ball. A grotesque chameleon-like change seemed to come over his whole being. He distorted his body to one of a chronic cripple, his lower jaw dropped and his face took on the expression of an imbecile. John had a great need to shock and disgust people and certainly shocked me on occasions like this. Of course when his mates were around, he was the star turn, appealing as he did to the sick side of their natures. Although I found John's humour really embarrassing, it was usually done so subtly that the fall guy on most occasions was unaware that he was having the mickey taken out of him, so no harm was done—and life was certainly never dull.

During the third year in college I started to be plagued with stomach pains. I tried very hard to ignore them hoping that they would go away, as I do with most problems, but they wouldn't oblige. Much to my dismay I found I was having to take the odd day or two off quite frequently. My work was suffering and I found that I was missing out on my training at a very crucial point. As it happened I wasn't all keen on paying my doctor a visit even at the worst of times, being a great believer in curing myself. One beautiful sunny afternoon, John and I finished college and decided to pay Stuart a visit. Stuart wasn't in but his flat-mates let us inside. We were very happy just be be alone together. We began to make mad, passionate love to each other, when I shrieked and found myself doubled up in excruciating agony on the bed. I must say that the timing was most inconvenient! I had never seen John look so worried. Panic—what on earth could be causing it? Wind? I always blamed any pain on wind. Well this wind was more like a hurricane and I could tell it was not about to subside. The pains grew worse, and I really started to panic at that point. My first thought was that I wanted my mum. I knew I had to get home as soon as possible. John virtually carried me to the station and bundled me on to the train. On my arrival at home, my mother opened the front door, took one look at me and rushed to the telephone. 'Hello, doctor? Could you come round at once please. I think my daughter is very poorly.' Within half an hour the doctor arrived, examined me briefly and phoned for an ambulance. I was on my way to the local cottage hospital with sirens wailing. It all happened so quickly, I really didn't know if I was on my head or my heels. I do remember one thing though, and that was to insist that my mother got in touch with John to let him know where I was and why. I was much more worried about him than I was about myself.

On arrival at the hospital I was informed that my symptoms were those of a grumbling appendix and that I had to stay in hospital under observation for the following two weeks. Well, I thought, how boring. All that melodrama for my appendix, and a grumbling one at that, what a let down. It was my first time as a patient in hospital and I enjoyed every moment of it, the luxury of being able to stay in bed all day and without feeling guilty. To receive so much love and attention, especially from John, was very welcome, so I made the most of the situation and lay back with my grapes and chocolates and my better humoured appendix with a smile on my face.

It was very difficult for John to visit me as often as he and I wished, but the first occasion upset me a great deal. I hated being separated from him and had dreamed of this visit day and night. When visiting time approached I was a bundle of nerves, sitting up in bed dressed in my best nightie, cheeks flushed with excitement, awaiting the great event. The bell rang out through the wards heralding visiting time. Friends and relatives of my fellow patients rushed in clasping bunches of brightly coloured flowers and brown paper bags of fruit and sweets. The expressions on their faces were full of eagerness and hope. Following the first rush of visitors everything went very quiet, people speaking in whispers to each other. I was still sitting up in my bed, the flush of my cheeks changing rapidly from excitement to embarrassment as the minutes ticked by and there was still no sign of John. I just couldn't believe it. 'How could he?' I thought 'I'll never speak to him again!' Just as I was about to burst into uncontrollable tears, a very readily recognizable head and hair-cut peered blindly around the door. Glasses were quickly sneaked on and (eureka!) at last he recognized me. I was thrilled. I would be able to tell him so much. We could have a whole hour together. But no, guess who was with him as he made his way red-faced to my bed? None other than George in all his glory. They were such a sight, but not for my sore eyes. That was when I really burst into tears. I will never forget the expression on George's face. Poor George. He had only come along to keep John company, at John's request. He had arrived with a broad grin spread across his face and my answer to that had been to break down crying. I should imagine his thoughts at that time were that he would never even begin to understand girls.

When John had realized how sensitively I was reacting to the situation he hurriedly bundled a confused George out of the ward and began to comfort me. All's well that ends well so they say. Making up for lost time we began to hold hands, and kiss as respectably as possible under the circumstances. When finally the bell tolled announcing that time was up, John said his goodbyes for himself and for the rejected George, and off the two of them went for egg and chips with my mother before catching the train back to Liverpool.

The days go by so slowly my mind held in suspense,
Why must this be when I can see the feeling so intense?
The future holds the magic of my thoughts these passing days
The planning actions of my mind just wither in the haze.
Time is wasted longing for the bud to flower and bloom.
Waiting, hoping, anticipating what might be happening soon.
Possibility is just a game played in fantasy throughout
Why must this be withheld within. What is it all about?
If only I could touch the flower and feel its beauty in my strife
I could be at ease and aim to please the pleasure of my life.

3

The Liverpool Scene

At this time John was having a wonderful time painting.
Stuart's influence on him grew very strong. All his inhibitions, brought about by the discipline of Lettering,
were gone and he threw himself naturally into an orgy
of oil paint, sand, sawdust, in fact anything he could lay
his hands on to create paintings that were truly individual.
John was in his element during this period. The only dark
cloud on his horizon was the Lettering exam that he knew
he would have to pass at the end of the year. If he failed
that he would definitely be out on his ear. If John was
worried he was marvellous at concealing it.

Then Allan Williams, a young, stocky, bearded friend
of Stuart's rose out of the dust like a phoenix into the
lives of John and the boys at this time. Although John
was immersed in his painting, his keenest interest was still
music. The boys continued to practise and perfect the
numbers they had been learning, the only problem was the
lack of opportunity to show off their talents. Allan Williams provided that for them in his coffee bar the Jacaranda. The Jac, as it was so fondly called by all who
entered its portals was a coffee bar famous for its bacon
butties. Down the narrow stairs to the basement was another world. My first impression was that of Dante's
Inferno. The heat, sweat and noise nearly knocked you
over with their power as you struggled and shoved to
descend the narrow heaving stairs.

The music that pulsated upwards, almost as if it were
desperately trying to escape the stifling confines of the

basement, was from a steel band. Not rock and roll, but a black steel band and they were marvellous! The atmosphere was electric—they were great and the only band of their kind in the area. Now at this point my memory fails me, but I think the boys hung around the Jac so often and pestered Allan so much that he finally weakened and let them have a blast for a night so that they could put their money and their guitars where their mouths were.

If Stuart hadn't been such a good friend of Allan's, I believe Allan would have turned a deaf ear to this request. For John was always cadging either food or money from Allan, and I'm sure he wondered what on earth he was letting himself in for. When eventually he gave in and allowed them their first public appearance, it was to a rather disgruntled audience. 'Who the hell are they, Allan?' 'Rubbish!' 'We want the steel band back.' 'God almighty, they really are bloody awful!' That's just a sample of the initial comments thrown at them by kids who later were to become their most avid fans.

Allan was soon to become a very firm supporter of the Beatles. His ears and intuition told him even in those very amateur, raw, early days that these lads definitely had something special. It wasn't their appearances that instilled this confidence in him, for there couldn't have been a scruffier group of musicians anywhere in Liverpool. And it definitely wasn't their stage presence. They didn't know what that was. In fact their foul language would have sent many a teenager's parents into a screaming fit if they had heard them in full flow.

It was a certain magic—so indefinable as to be almost non-existent at times—until they started playing their guitars and singing their harmonies. That was the moment the tingle went up the spine, the first stages of addiction. It was a very far cry from the neatness and uniformity of the Shadows, who were way up in the popularity charts at the time. So totally opposite was their image that it seemed unbelievable that the kids and teeny-boppers would take even a second look at the Beatles, never mind follow them to the ends of the earth. The only uniformity that they adhered to at that stage was in their own choice of attire. Unpressed jeans, black T-shirts and tennis plimps—usually dirty. Their hair was long and greased back at the sides but left at the front to fall casually onto their foreheads. Rough diamonds in every sense of the word compared to the Shadows' clean-cut, besuited image. They were young, rough and sexy. Their music was gutsy and raw, and with the help and guidance of Allan Williams, their limited experience was about to grow in a very exciting way.

With all the excitement of live performances I was beginning to find myself absorbed into a whole new lifestyle. John's perfect image of a woman was, I said earlier, Brigitte Bardot. I found myself fast becoming moulded into her style of dress and haircut. I had only recently gone through my change from secretary-bird to Bohemian when I met John, but under his influence another metamorphosis was taking place and this time the emphasis was on *oomph!* Long blonde hair (out came the Hiltone), tight black sweaters, tight short skirts, high-heeled pointed shoes, and to add the final touch, black fish-net stockings and suspenders. The only trouble with an outfit like that was that on many an occasion, when I had arranged to meet my beloved in Liverpool outside Lewis's store directly underneath the then controversial statue of a nude man, or outside Central Station or wherever, John would invariably turn up late and I was forever in danger of being picked up by the most unsavoury characters that Liverpool could offer.

I must have looked every inch like a Liverpool Totty— a prostitute—on the game. Attempting to look inconspicuous under those circumstances was impossible, and once again I fell prey to my own excruciating self-consciousness, until John arrived at my side, then all would be well again. If that was the way he wanted me to look then it was all right by me, but I must admit there was a shy, bespectacled, secretary-type trying to get out. It was much, much safer being inconspicuous.

When Allan took the Beatles under his wing, he also gave them the opportunity to air their talents in other dance-hall venues and clubs. John, finding home life with Mimi less than *avant garde*, decided to move into Stuart's flat with him, a decision that Mimi did her utmost to

'E-aar gerl how much?'

squash. But his mind was made up. He felt he had to cut the apron strings and please himself. I was to spend many a night in that flat with John—my mother believing me to be staying with Phyllis.

Although it was wonderful spending illicit nights away from home, we had terrible trouble trying to keep clean. It was impossible, no matter how hard we tried. The floor was filthy, in fact everything was covered with muck. If the electricity had been cut off or the supply of soap had run out we would wash in cold water and without light, emerging into the bright daylight of Liverpool and walking hand in hand to the city centre for breakfast looking, I suspect, like a couple of chimney sweeps. John didn't really care too much, but I had to return home and explain my appearance to my disbelieving mother. Oh, it was great fun! Looking like a fallen angel was one thing, but looking like a dirty fallen angel on the last train home to suburbia was quite another kettle of fish.

The lunchtime and dance-hall sessions were often very frightening experiences for me, mainly because the music lovers who followed the Beatles around were becoming more and more possessive about their chosen Beatle idol. And this, let me add, was in the very early stages of the group's career. I would accompany John on most of their gigs. Sometimes he would be petrified because he had heard on the grapevine that he was to be kicked in by the local Teds. Their Judies (Birds) were taking too much notice of the Beatles and the Teds weren't going to stand for it. The real danger areas were Bootle and Litherland town halls and Garston. All the local hard knocks would be waiting to put the boot into Lennon, McCartney, Harrison and Sutcliffe. The joy of performing was well and truly knocked out of them on those occasions and sheer unadulterated panic set in. I, on the other hand, being the only female connected with the Beatles at the beginning, was in a horribly vulnerable position. The fanatical John Lennon followers did not take kindly to me. I was a threat to their fantasies and dreams. The most dangerous place for me in those days was the ladies' loo. I honestly thought that once I had entered, I wouldn't get out again in one piece, or worse still that I would never be seen alive again.

My solution to this was to keep a very low profile and keep my mouth firmly shut. I would smile in such a friendly way, and if it was necessary for me to speak I would adopt my best Liverpool accent in case they thought that I was putting on airs and graces. I was really afraid of someone picking an argument with me. I was definitely no match at all for those girls. They could have killed me as soon as look at me.

From the first appearance at the Jacaranda, John, Paul, George and Stuart went from strength to strength. They were minus a drummer, that was true, and to begin with they played with borrowed amplifiers. Allan gave them regular gigs, lunchtime sessions mainly—don't forget we were all still at college or school. Everything seemed to fit in beautifully, although needless to say our academic studies took second place to the excitement of live performances. During this period Allan Williams' interests also extended to two or three other Liverpool groups. He wasn't their manager in the accepted sense, but he did help them in any way that he could, acquiring work for them in the numerous clubs and dance-halls in Liverpool and even on the other side of the water, would you believe! In recompense Allan would, at the end of the day, keep back enough expenses for his trouble. He was quite an enigmatic man, a character full of enthusiasm, ambition and boundless energy. The man, in fact, who was responsible for putting the Liverpool sounds on the map.

The Jac as I have said, was dark, sweaty and alive, alive with sounds and God only knows what else. Office clerks, shop assistants, factory workers, students, layabouts, black, white, yellow, coffee-coloured were all squashed together into the steaming, vibrating Jacaranda melting pot. When the boys played with their borrowed amplifiers, their microphones were tied to brush handles held at the base of the so-called stage by ardent, ever-accommodating little Liverpool fans. It was a beautiful sight. Co-operation and communication held together by four scruffy young lads playing their hearts out, for peanuts. Although the idea of playing for money was important, the mere fact that they could play to an audience and create electricity between themselves and everyone else who heard their music was more than enough in those early stages to satisfy their young egos. They could begin to see the light at the end of the tunnel.

Enthusiasm and excitement mounted at the prospect of some sort of a career in the world of music. John had decided, now that he had tasted the show biz scene, that this was very definitely the life for him. All the ideas that everyone else had had for him of making an impact on the art world faded into the back of beyond with incredible rapidity, and with almost no regret at all. John's Aunt Mimi, however, was distraught and agitated at the prospect of her charge racing headlong into an unpredictable future armed only with an old guitar, with no qualifications, and virtually penniless. Her view of his future couldn't have been blacker at that time. A famous quote from Mimi was, 'It's all very nice playing the guitar John, but you will never make any money at it!' Poor Mimi's advice from the heart fell on very deaf ears, and thank goodness it did.

It was during this particular period that life at college was warming up for the end of Summer term exams. One of those exams was to be John's last chance to prove himself worthy of staying on at the college. There was a slight chance that John would scrape through, with a little help from his friends, until Allan Williams dropped a bombshell. 'Lads,' he said, 'Larry Parnes and Billy Fury are coming up from London to hold an audition. Parnes needs a backing group for Billy on his next tour.' From that moment all hell was let loose. When I saw John after he had heard this earth-shattering news you would have thought that he had won the pools. 'Christ, Cyn, do you know what this means? An audition for Larry Parnes and Billy Fury. Bloody hell I don't believe it. *Christ*, it's too much. Billy Fury, just imagine it! Backing Billy Fury. Yahoo!'

Sheer unadulterated joy shone from John's face as he was relating this marvellous news to me. He was like a child who had lost a penny and found a pound note. There wasn't any doubt in John's mind at that moment that they could possibly fail this chance-of-a-lifetime audition. His optimism was boundless. The fact that none of the boys rated Billy Fury in their personal top ten didn't even enter his head. Billy Fury had made it and now they were on their way, thanks to Allan Williams. During the weeks before the audition John, Paul, George and Stuart practised until their fingers nearly dropped off. But when the full impact of the situation sank in, they began to get nervous. For a start they didn't have a drummer. Then Stuart was worried—understandably so since his new found prowess at the bass guitar left a great deal to be desired. I think for the first time they took a critical look at themselves and they really weren't sure what they could do to improve their appearance and musical standard. They realized that they had to rely on their own particular brand of magic; they couldn't *afford* to do anything else. When the fateful day finally arrived, the adrenaline was running very fast.

The boys had scouted around Liverpool for the best stand-in drummer they could find, and they were successful. They were all set. The stage clothes, instead of dirty jeans, black T-shirts and scruffy off-white plimsolls were, (wait for it) clean jeans, clean black T-shirts and scruffy off-white plimsolls. Their hair was combed and greased to perfection. To me they looked beautiful. Their faces were fresh and alive with a mixture of excitement and fear. I was so proud of them I could have cried.

At the audition, which was being held in the basement of Allan's club, The Blue Angel, the tension was mounting. The drummer was conspicuous by his absence. The boys busied themselves, tuning their guitars with shaking hands, discussing how they were going to stand, smoking ciggies as if they were about to go out of fashion, deciding what movements they should make, if any, to impress the visiting stars of entertainment and show business. They were all so innocent and young in their attitude it was lovely. It was into this scene, with a backcloth of a dingy Liverpool basement in the process of being decorated, that the VIPs eventually made their entrance. The sudden silence and atmosphere of expectation was extremely overpowering until Allan's introductions broke the spell. I think Allan was as nervous as the boys by this time and they all started talking at once. Comparisons are odious, and I was very biased at the time, but the expensively dressed suavity of the visiting stars couldn't hold a candle then to the appearance of those four lads. Billy Fury was quite to the point of being sullen throughout the ensuing proceedings. He hardly said a word, let alone showed any enthusiasm. Larry Parnes sat and listened intently to the boys as they sang and played their hearts out. I sat inconspicuously in one corner with my fingers and legs tightly crossed, watching, scrutinizing the faces of the audience for signs of disapproval or, God willing, enthusiasm.

I suppose auditioning someone is a little like buying a house. If you show enthusiasm the vendors might put the price up. As it happened the boys did not secure the job. Larry Parnes' reasoning was that Stuart's bass playing was definitely not up to performance standard, but, and it was a very big but, he was prepared to take the rest of them on. He was impressed. Following a deep discussion amongst themselves and Allan, John refused point blank. 'If Stuart isn't with us then they can forget it.' And that was that as far as John was concerned. His loyalty to Stuart was marvellous, and he was immediately backed up by Paul and George. Stuart, on the other hand, was feeling incredibly low. He did his utmost to dissuade them from their final decision and my heart went out to him. He felt, quite naturally, that their opportunity to make a name for themselves had been ruined by his lack of talent. Allan sat next to Stuart and suggested that he showed them his other talent, portraiture. Stuart refused at first but with more encouragement proceeded to sketch Billy Fury and Larry Parnes. Stuart always carried an old canvas bag with him containing a sketchbook and the necessary materials for on-the-spot drawings of subjects that inspired him, and which he could utilize later in his oil-painting. I can't say that Stuart was inspired at all by the subjects confronting him. He was too full of disappointment and remorse for artistic inspiration to break through, but he proceeded to work on and finish his charcoal portraits of his sitters, much to their delight and surprise.

Parnes liked the Beatles (minus Stuart) a lot and before leaving informed Allan that he would keep them in mind if anything else suitable turned up. There were other Liverpool groups taking part in this audition, groups with far more experience than the Beatles, well-established Liverpool groups. Cass and the Cassanovas, Rory Storm and the Hurricanes, Derry and the Seniors. Rory Storm had just come back from a very successful season at a Butlin's holiday camp in North Wales, and the drummer for the group was the one and only Richard Starkey, alias Ringo Starr. A mere twinkle in the Beatles' eyes at that time. I must admit that even though the turnout of the other groups was far superior to the boys' as far as clothes and equipment were concerned, like Larry Parnes I only had eyes for them.

Although there was an air of disappointment following us all around for some time, the anti-climax wasn't too bad. After all, they were instilled with a greater confidence than ever before. They had been judged the winners of that particular contest and against all odds. They couldn't be bad. What they really needed now was a steady supply of work and with it a steady supply of money for better equipment. Sad to say, though, that wasn't to be for quite a while.

Paul was still at school, George left and became an apprentice electrician at a large Liverpool department store and John, well John still had his bloody lettering exam to do, didn't he? What a let down when he could have been earning one hundred pounds a week with his name in lights to boot.

As for my relationship with John, in between college, playing town hall gigs and night-time sessions at the Jac, John and I still had time for each other. We were very close, probably closer then than before or since. Wherever John went I was by his side unless he thought it too dangerous for me. If they were playing in an area where knives and fists flashed, as frequently was the case, then I would stay away. He had enough to worry about then without the added worry of me being beaten up as well. Although I frequently went along to fairly seedy venues with him, I must admit I was scared out of my wits. The atmosphere was electric with vibrant, aggressive, sweaty bodies crammed and seething in some small dance-hall. One look in the wrong direction, at the wrong person could, and frequently did, set off a chain reaction of events which

45

would make your hair stand on end. It was like sitting on a time bomb. On such an occasion I would wonder what the hell I was doing there in the first place. I knew in my bones that life would never be dull when I first fell for John, but this was definitely something else. Where would it all end, I thought to myself. I would only have to look at John and the boys to find the answer. Their music, their vibrance, their aura was irresistible and willingly I was being pulled along in the slip-stream of their talent. I was almost as much a part of it as they were and once you have stepped onto a fast-moving vehicle, you've just got to think twice before stepping off.

Then there were the amusing times that John and I spent with Aunt Mimi. She would always make sure that we were well fed—masses of chips, eggs, sausages, plates stacked high with bread and butter, endless cups of tea and many more questions. 'John you look terrible. Just look at the state you're in; you look a disgrace; you should be ashamed of yourself! Cynthia, what is going to become of him? I really despair when I think about him. Can't you persuade him to leave that stinking flat that he is dossing in? What's the name of that scruffy fellow who he's sharing the flat with, if you could call it a flat?'

There'd be a pause for two seconds just enough time for me to reply, 'Well you should know John by now, Mimi.'

'Yes, that's what I'm worried about Cyn,' Mimi would continue. 'He doesn't look as though he's had a square meal in days and neither do you, if it comes to that. What on earth do you two get up to?'

At this point in the proceedings John would jump in to save my face, changing the subject beautifully. 'The garden's looking great, Mimi, the meal was fantastic, and how about another cup of tea?'

When all the food was eaten and the conversation exhausted we would take our leave, but not before Mimi had taken me to one side and pleaded with me to try and persuade 'the stupid fool' to return home. She was so worried about him that she couldn't sleep at night and, needless to say, her ulcer was acting up again. I would reply that I would do my best, but John really was his own man and old enough to look after himself. End of visit and back to square one for Mimi.

From time to time John and I would also drop in on Paul's lovely dad. We would never fail to receive a warm welcome from Jim. Paul's father had lost his beloved wife Mary quite a few years before I ever came into contact with the McCartney family and he had brought up the two young boys, Paul and Michael. Mike of course is now known as Mike Macgear of Scaffold fame. The warmth I experienced whenever I entered the modest home of this talented family, which was in Forthlyn Road, Allerton, was wonderful. Jim was a father in a million. The cheerful way he coped with a situation that many a man would have run away from was admirable. Usually Jim would greet us at the front door with a tea towel in one hand and a saucepan in the other, his shirt sleeves neatly rolled up around his elbows and an apron tied around his waist. In the kitchen we would be confronted with chaos, a wonderful homely chaos. The chip pan would be on and the tempting smell of bacon and eggs would fill our nostrils. Jim had only to look at our faces and the extra potatoes would be chipped and more bacon and eggs would sizzle away in the pan. Before we knew it we would be sitting down to what was for us a right royal banquet.

I always enjoyed my visits to Jim. Always full of enthusiasm towards the boys and their music, Jim had himself been a member of a very successful jazz band in his youth. It was about this time that I found a very close female friend. I had really been missing silly female gossip. My great friend Phyllis's mother had died very suddenly and very tragically of cancer and with a young brother and sister still at school and a father out at work she felt she should give up her idea of becoming a teacher and earn some money to help out on the home front. This had meant of course that I now saw very little of her. We still kept in touch and I really did miss her friendship. I always seemed to be in the company of fellers which was all very well, but you can't beat a good old natter with your girlfriend. But then, through Paul, I met Dorothy. Dot was lovely, seventeen years old, slim, short blonde hair (not out of a bottle), and the most attractive pixie face you have ever seen. Dot was such a gentle soul, shes spoke almost in a whisper, blushed frequently and idolized Paul.

Apart from the fact that we immediately got on like a house on fire, we had one very big thing in common—our adoration of the Beatles and their music. They could do nothing wrong in our eyes so there was a great affinity between us. Most important, at last I had company when the boys were playing. I think Dot was Paul's first serious girl-friend. She worked on the dispensing side of a chemist in the outskirts of Liverpool and lived at home with her mother and father. Dot's parents were very strict and so she didn't see as much of Paul as I did of John. Mind you, if my father had still been alive I doubt very much if my relationship with John would ever have survived. He was very strait-laced, my dad. I remember when I was only fifteen, a very scruffy lad took a great shine to me. He looked a real layabout and I wasn't the least bit interested in him until he wrote me a long loving letter. I was so impressed with his letter which was written exquisitely with a very fine nib, that I became curious. I found it hard to equate the appearance and manner of him with the beautiful letter. So, being the type of person that takes nothing at face value, I thought I would like to find out a bit more about him. Unfortunately, I never got the chance. He arrived at my home, one evening, in his best Teddy-boy outfit and asked to see me. I happened to be out at the time, so my mother, feeling sorry for him, asked him inside to wait. Five minutes later my father arrived home from work, was confronted by this unlikely lad, and, taking him for a removal man delivering some of my mother's sale-room acquisitions, he gave him ten bob! He honestly thought that the lad was waiting for a tip. Neither my mother or I ever enlightened my father as to the real purpose of his visit and obviously it never crossed his mind that his daughter would have had anything remotely to do with a boy of his type. Poor lad, he must have been so confused, and that was the last I ever saw of him.

4

The German Experience

John's mind was definitely not on his college work any longer and from that point of view his future looked decidedly uncertain. Needless to say, I worried enough for both of us, but could see no hope of his passing the Lettering papers since there was absolutely no incentive. Allan had signed an agreement with Larry Parnes to provide him with backing groups for his shows and the Beatles were set for their first big chance. The news that the group was to back Johnny Gentle on a tour of Inverness and Galashiels in Scotland was received by John with great enthusiasm and was the final nail in the coffin for his examinations. So it was that I found myself in desperation setting about Part II of his Lettering paper myself. This was the part which a student had to complete untutored and within a certain time limit. Confronted with a very dog eared piece of paper, smudged with pencil and paint, a great blob obliterating the central area of the lettering altogether, I sat down on an orange box in Stuart's flat under a bare sixty-watt light bulb, armed with rubber, paint-brush and pencil, to do my best—John and Stuart hanging over my shoulder having hysterics and knowing, as I did, that I didn't stand a cat's chance in hell of saving him from being thrown out of college.

When the worst happened, John was not at all perturbed. Why should he be—all he could think of was touring with Johnny Gentle. The big time was on the horizon. They each received ten pounds a week which was far below their living expenses. In fact the whole experience gave the Beatles their first full unsavoury taste of life on the fringe of the pop business proper. One night stands; living out of a suitcase; fish and chips here, the odd unsavoury sausage roll there; tatty lodgings . . . the whole shebang! On top of this the promoter complained about their appearance and the drummer was definitely *not* a Lennon fan. But did all this put them off? Not likely, they thrived on it. Who the hell wanted a nine-to-five job when they could have all this? Their enthusiasm was boundless: 'What have you got lined up for us next, Al?' 'Come on, Al, we need the money, we need more work, try and get us fixed up with something, Al. Ah go on, Al.' Allan must have been harassed to death by those four scruffy individuals during that miserable period of transition.

I had to have my appendix cut out during the first heat wave we had had in years. Not a very pleasant experience, but catching up on lost time was my worse problem. I lost out on six weeks of college time while convalescing, and if I was to pass the National Diploma, I would have to work like the devil himself.

Allan, at this time, had a great disappointment. One of his prize possessions disappeared from the Liverpool scene —his steel band. Only after many inquiries did he find out that the band had been tempted away by the Germans. The steel band was in Hamburg doing very well, thank you. The answer to Allan's bewildered question, 'What the hell does Hamburg have to offer?' became clear over the following months. To the Beatles it was heaven sent; to Allan it was a whole new experience in proving his managerial finesse with men he found it almost impossible to communicate with. But his business sense told him that Hamburg had a great deal to offer him and his talented stable of Liverpool groups, despite the language barrier. So Allan packed his bags and off he went to investigate the German set-up. To cut a long story short, due to Allan's visit and subsequent business deals with a Hamburg club owner called Bruno Koschmider, the boys found themselves on their way to Hamburg to play nightly at the Kaiserkeller. But before they could go they had to find a drummer. As luck would have it a young lad called Pete Best was available. The boys had come into contact with

Pete when they played a few times at his mother's coffee bar which was in the basement of his house in a suburb of Liverpool, Haymans Green. Peter was quite a good drummer and enjoyed sitting in on their sessions whenever the Beatles played there. He was very handsome in a moody, sultry sort of way and hardly ever spoke or showed any enthusiasm. He reminded me at the time of a very young Jeff Chandler. The kids who frequented the coffee bar would sit and ogle him. He was very popular with the girls but seemed to lack the sense of humour that was such an integral part of the boys' make-up. In this sense he really didn't gel with their characters right from the very start. But they needed him and he was only too willing to join them.

Look out, you Krauts, here we come!

Parting from John was terrible. I hadn't been farther away from him than a twenty minute train journey since I met him. We were both incredibly excited about the German trip but the thought of separation was really awful. We promised each other that we would be faithful, that we would write to each other every day. It was a very loving parting. The thought of being stuck at home for goodness knows how many months without John made me feel very low and the only thing for me to do was to throw myself into my neglected art work. My mother was thrilled at the return of her prodigal daughter. She had never been over the moon about my relationship with John and although she didn't say anything I'm sure she was hoping that 'Out of sight out of mind' would prove to be the case.

As expected, the following five months dragged beyond belief. 'Mr Postman look and see if there's a letter in your bag for me' was definitely my theme song during those lonely times. I thought of all those beautiful blonde Germanic girls and doubts and fears would crowd in on me nightly until his letters arrived in the morning, and true to his word he didn't once let me down. God only knows what the postman thought on his daily round. 'Postman, postman don't be slow, I'm in love with Cyn so go man go,' was typical. The envelopes were covered in loving verse and kisses would almost obliterate the address. John's letters would tell me how dreadful their living conditions

51

were. How the German opportunist Bruno Koschmider was making a packet out of them in his clubs for very little in return. That their living quarters consisted of three filthy rooms, furnished only with camp beds and blankets. That the washing and toilet facilities were appalling. That their rooms were situated behind a cinema screen, the cinema having been converted from an old theatre, leaving room for the boys' sparse furnishings in the disused dressing rooms.

The Indra, until their arrival on the scene, had been very popular for its risque girlie shows. It was all low lighting, plush furnishings and seductive music. The small, cramped stage did not lend itself to the boys' antics and neither did the audience. They wanted their girls back. Although John's letters frequently bemoaned the situation, I could tell he was enjoying every little bit of the experience. It definitely beat lettering and college life and the only thing he was missing was me, which made me feel marvellous and very miserable at the same time. Such reassurance, however, meant that my work definitely improved. My tutors seemed to be pleased about the absence of the love of my life.

The Reeperbahn, where the Indra was situated, was a hundred times less salubrious than our own Soho. Sex, booze, music and pills were the name of the game and those young 'innocent' lads were right in the middle of it all. They worked very long hours in those German clubs and it was the best thing that could have happened to them as far as their music was concerned, improving as they did way beyond my wildest dreams. Their technique, their staying power, the sheer guts and enthusiasm that went into their every performance, the sound that they produced—all this stretched out and tore at your very being. It was so total in its concept that no one could escape it, least of all one Astrid Kirschner, and Klaus Voorman, her boy-friend at the time. Astrid was a photographer, a very beautiful girl whose family was upper-class German and whose ideas were as way out as the Beatles themselves. The moment Astrid set eyes on the boys and heard for herself the incredible sounds that they were producing she became totally addicted and made sure that

52

she was introduced to them. Naturally the boys were very flattered and John's letters were full of Astrid and Klaus— particularly her way of dress, her *avant garde* way of life and her marvellous photography. In fact as far as I could see, the sun shone out of Astrid's backside and I was definitely not Astrid's number one fan at that time. I was sure that if Astrid was such a fantastic girl then it would not be very long before I would be receiving a 'Dear Cynthia' letter.

How the imagination runs riot. The truth of the matter was, as I was to learn later, that Astrid had fallen hopelessly in love with Stuart. She fell at first for Stuart's James Dean image. Although he was small in stature he did have a marked charisma and a slight resemblance to James Dean more in characteristic poses than looks. For a start, he was short-sighted, but unlike John and I he wasn't so vain that he would do without his glasses. Instead, he wore very dark prescription lenses in a black frame, all very mysterious and very fitting for a member of a rock band.

Meanwhile, back at the ranch, I was spending a small fortune in Woolworths. The reason being that John and I did not have photographs of each other. Each week I would dress up in my most seductive outfit and squash into the tiny photo booth trying my best to look loving, longing and seductive. Scruffy little kids would pull the curtain aside and yell, 'Eeaar, gerl, hey look at gorgeous Gussy then! Hey, gerl, your knickers are falling down,' and so on. As you can imagine, the desired effect was never achieved and when the photographs finally dropped into the slot after they had been developed they were always a terrible let-down. The sickly grin, the expression of suppressed anger were a million miles away from what I had been hoping for.

John was doing the same thing in a booth in Hamburg, minus the scruffy kids. His photographs for me were hilarious. Each time I received a letter I hoped that there would be a photograph of him that was fit to display. No way! Hunchbacks would grin insanely at me; grotesque positions and expressions would leer at me, each one worse and more horrific than the last. Not one could I look on with loving adoration without bursting into fits of uncon-

53

trollable giggles. Even the lens of a camera was John's audience and he'd do his best to shock that, if it was possible. From the mood of his letters, John seemed to be changing. His cruel, caustic wit was still very much in evidence but all the pent-up destructive aggression was waning. He had no time to dwell on his misfortunes, and lived for the moment. All his energy was being used to create the sound that was to turn the world of music on its ear.

It wasn't long after I had settled down to the idea of coping with life on my own that news arrived that they were on their way home. Apparently it had just been high spirits that had created the scene that sent Koschmider scurrying off to the German police for help, resulting in George and Paul being locked up in the local nick. There were no charges preferred against them, but they were packed off back to England the following day. George, in fact, was too young to have a work permit and on that score alone they definitely blotted their copy books for further work in Germany.

The truth of the matter was, as John told me, that before the 'incident' occurred they had broken their contract with Koschmider by playing in a rival club—the Top Ten Club which was also in the Reeperbahn. Tony Sheridan was their star attraction and the boys really dug him. He had a fantastic voice and stage presence which really impressed the boys. So when they had time off, which wasn't often, they would sneak into the Top Ten to listen to him. On one occasion that they sat in with him, there was a spy in the audience. The result was that Koschmider was looking for an excuse to vent his anger on the boys for their indiscretion. He had his petty revenge when they were messing around in their rooms with a candle and set fire to some old sacks. This was enough for the German authorities to come down on them hard and days later they arrived home almost as penniless as they had left. But the most important fact remained: their music had matured beyond all recognition.

As far as I was concerned, this unexpected premature return, for whatever reason, good or bad, delighted me. But the boys were disgruntled and very angry. The whole stupid affair had left an acrid taste in their mouths, especially as they were just moving into top gear with their German audiences. The worry of their being banned forever from Hamburg weighed very heavily on them. They loved the place. The atmosphere, the freedom of expression, the magic they felt as their audiences became more and more ecstatic over their earthy, belting music and crazy antics made Liverpool look like a dead city. After Hamburg anything would have appeared dull.

The Liverpool fans had not forgotten them, however, and welcomed them home as only Liverpudlians can do. The new sound that they were producing had the kids falling about in the dance-halls and clubs. They had never before been confronted with such a magnetic combination of sheer brute force and magnitude of sound. The whole experience left them reeling, drained of emotion, and panting for more. The Beatles were growing from strength to strength. Dance-halls were crammed full of adoring screaming fans, boys and girls alike. Yet they still missed the 'Fatherland'. They liked the Germans, at least the ones they had come into contact with in the clubs. The boozy, rough, raucous nights peppered with guttural shouts of 'Mak Show'. Crates of beer arriving on stage with the compliments of the roughest looking character in the club on the condition that they drank them all, or else. Fights breaking out at the drop of a hat. Fights that most of us only see on the screen with table and chairs flying through the air to the accompaniment of Mack The Knife. Oh yes, they loved Hamburg. Where else could they get that sort of excitement and get paid for it?

They desperately wanted to go back, but this time to the Top Ten Club which was run by Peter Eckhorn, an honourable man by comparison with Koschmider. Peter was very keen to employ the boys but the fact remained that the police had sent them home. Allan Williams came to the rescue once more. He wrote to the German Consulate praising the boys' background, musical ability, and personalities, explaining how they had been exploited, as indeed he had been by the very unprofessional Bruno Koschmider. He asked for work permits, for work that was very much above board, with a very honourable German businessman,

55

namely Peter Eckhorn. The letter did the trick. Thanks to Allan, they were on their way again before very long, this time a much happier and more confident group of Beatles.

I was happier too, for this time I was to visit them in Hamburg and Dot was to accompany me. We were so excited, we were fit to bust. It was the first time that either of us had set foot outside the British Isles. London was the farthest that I had ever been from Liverpool. It was so hard to contain our ever-growing excitement. We would meet frequently in coffee bars and talk for hours on end, endlessly puffing away, neither of us inhaling but both of us needing something to do with our hands to stop them fidgeting and twitching with excitement. We were just living for the moment when we would step onto that boat-train bound for the Hook of Holland.

Dot had a great deal of difficulty in persuading her parents that all would be well on the trip, but a solemn promise of good behaviour and constant pleading wore them down and eventually they gave her their permission.

Paul's Dad Jim and my mother saw us off on the boat-train. It was an overnight train and although we were both consumed with excitement we were really a couple of very green teenagers. Armed with our cheese butties and thermos flasks of tea, the world seemed our oyster. We waved like mad and yelled our last goodbyes to Jim and my mother as the night train pulled slowly and powerfully out of Lime Street Station. The dim lights of the station flickered and grew fainter in the distance as the engine picked up speed. We were on our way! 'Hamburg, Dot. We're on our way to bloody Hamburg! I can't believe it!'

The idyllic image of our handsome heroes waiting for us with open arms on the platform of a foreign station, all misty and romantic, kept us occupied. The only thing we really lacked was food. We were literally starving as the train from Holland to Hamburg didn't have a dining-car and the only opportunity we had of obtaining food was when we pulled into a station. The problem though, was that we were both too nervous to get off the train in case it pulled out and left one of us on the platform. We were such a couple of muggins. Neither of us spoke a word of any other language than English, so we could get no idea how long the train would be stationary.

Our arrival at Hamburg station was a far cry from our romantic imaginings. When finally the train came to a halt, it was a very early morning that saw two bedraggled, travel-weary young girls virtually falling out onto the platform (after experiencing great difficulty in opening the door), starving, exhausted and looking a lot less glamorous than we had hoped. For this momentous reunion, we were greeted, not by our gallant heroes, but by a length of platform that would have daunted even a champion long-distance runner. The suitcases felt as though they had been filled with lead. Certainly we were not a pretty sight, but neither was the vision from the farthest reaches of the platform of two equally bedraggled baggy-eyed creatures, reeking of alcohol, leaping and bounding towards us like a couple of lunatics. But what a reunion! Hugs, kisses and shouts of joy. We had the platform to ourselves and it was a great show we put on.

Paul and John were overjoyed at our safe arrival. They had been playing until two in the morning, and had been too excited to go to bed. The pills and booze they had been stuffing into themselves had heightened their senses beyond our reason, and they overwhelmed us with their non-stop chat and frenzied excitement. Neither of us had seen them in this state before, but we were soon to get accustomed to the reasoning behind this need for artificial highs. Two weeks in Hamburg and we were all on them.

For my part, I was so happy to be with John again. To be in a town that didn't have my name and number; to be free of any restrictions. I felt wonderful; a new exciting world to discover; a strange language so unfamiliar to my ears forcing itself into my consciousness; I was consumed by a willingness to accept virtually everything that was put in my path.

It had been previously arranged that I was to stay with Astrid and her mother in Eims Butteler Strasse and Dot was to stay with Paul on a house-boat owned by the Top Ten Club's lavatory attendant—Rosa, a great favourite with the boys. So following an enormous breakfast of bacon and eggs at the Seaman's Mission on the Hamburg

57

docks, we went our separate ways. It was with great trepidation that I went to meet Astrid for the first time. She sounded as though she could run rings around me in every way—looks, talent, personality, the lot. My confidence was at a very low ebb until I was welcomed into her home. Astrid was beautiful, not just physically beautiful but in every respect. Her mode of dress was simple: jeans, black polo-neck sweater and black leather jacket. Her hair was cropped short and layered and she had a full mouth and enormous eyes, enhanced by her very professional use of eye make-up. Her mouth was intentionally understated with a very pale pink lipstick. The overall effect was a knock-out, totally individual, as was her character. I warmed to her immediately and the language difficulties didn't even occur. We felt as though we had known each other for years. What a marvellous way to start a holiday, and a friendship. Astrid's home was a very substantially built three-storey house in the suburbs of Hamburg, very tastefully furnished with antiques, Persian carpets, chandeliers and so on. But when Astrid showed me her room, it was like walking into the future. The walls and ceiling were covered with silver foil and everything else was black. The bed-spread was black velvet, the sheets black satin. From the ceiling concealed spotlights were strategically placed to focus artistically onto the various modern sketches and paintings that hung on the silver walls, which in turn glittered and gleamed in the reflected light. A beautiful dried flower and branch arrangement was also spotlit and provided enough natural form and colour to break up the starkness of the room's lines. To me the effect was breathtaking, especially when I thought of my own bedroom at home with its uniform dressing-table and floral nylon bedspread. Yuck! Astrid was really ahead of her time.

Those two weeks in Hamburg were an eye-opener to me in every way. And it was such a happy, carefree, loving time for John and myself. Our meeting on the day after my arrival and after a good night's rest was idyllic. The sun shone and everything looked and smelled wonderful. John's attention was totally taken up with me. He took great delight in showing me around his Hamburg, a bus-

58

tling port full of excitement and colour, not unlike
Liverpool in many ways. The German language seemed not
unlike the nasal almost guttural true scouse accent, in fact
I should think it would come very easily to a Liverpudlian.
I believe that was why the boys fitted in so well with the
whole scheme of things there. My tour included such sights
as the port with its liners towering above us with their
beautiful shapes silhouetted against a back-cloth of cranes,
sea birds and azure sky. The ferries, again so like our own
on the Mersey, streamed in and out with little regard for
the rest of us. They knew exactly where they were going,
unlike us mere mortals who observed them with such delight.

In complete contrast to the majesty of those great queens
of the open sea, John decided that I needed educating in
other directions. Hand in hand, he led me into the heart of
Hamburg's Soho, down one particular narrow Strasse. It
really *was* an education for me. I was amazed at what I
saw! Each house was about three storeys high and on the
ground floor of each building, large picture windows overlooked the narrow cobbled street. And seated in each
window, in various stages of undress, were the street ladies
of Hamburg, selling their wares as blatantly as a barrow
boy would sell his goods in an open market place. As we
wandered past, their loud voices invited potential customers to come and try out the goods. While shouting they
would stroke their bodies, showing off their most sensual
attributes in no uncertain manner. John was so amused by
the expression on my face. My reaction to all that I was
witnessing was just what he had hoped. Hoylake didn't
have anything like this down its side-streets. It was just
like watching 'What the butler saw' without having to pay
for it and without inhibition. What an experience! If my
mother could see me now! In broad daylight too!

The Top Ten Club, where the boys played nightly,
was an immense place. It had nothing of the intimacy of
the London discos. It was almost utilitarian in its concept.
Bright lights glared down onto a clientele of a very mixed
variety. Raucous beer-swilling rough-necks sat within reach
of middle-class, middle-aged groups. Teenagers, dressed in
the latest fashions, rubbed shoulders with very nasty knife-

toting gangsters and sailors, men on leave from the forces. You name them, I could pick them out for you. The Reeperbahn attracts men like a candle attracts the flimsy moth . . . and many got their fingers burned. Fights were frequent and the German police, so unlike our own British bobbies, would swoop in on any disturbance with the alacrity of a storm trooper. Sirens howling, dressed in uniforms not unlike those of the infamous SS, they weren't a pretty sight. In fact they put the fear of God into me. Guns were always at the ready, their ominous muzzles gleaming in the bright lights of the club and any trouble was soon put to an end without a great deal of opposition. The tables and chairs in the Top Ten were the type that one would find in the average works' canteen. With the nightly breakages, I suppose anything more luxurious would have cost them a fortune to replace. So it was in this atmosphere and under those conditions that the boys earned their money and gained their invaluable experience in those early, formative years.

The Beatles' living quarters, although a great improvement on the previous pit they had to live in, were awful by most people's standards. They had one room approximately ten feet square. As far as I can remember the walls were painted in a very drab, dark, sludgy colour. The only window in evidence was minute and even that didn't give them a glimpse of the outside world as it overlooked a wide, dingy, staircase that led to the club. They were living in battery-hen conditions, bed/work, work/bed, with a couple of meals in between to keep them alive. They slept in bunk-beds which took up most of the room, altogether a miserable little dump. But they were happier than they had ever been. The only bone of contention was the fact that Pete just wasn't fitting in. His drumming was fine, for what was required of him, but as far as his character and humour was concerned he was a misfit. A good lad, but a loner who brooded a great deal on his own, certainly no exhibitionist.

I was staying in comparative luxury in the top flat of Astrid's home, a lovely self-contained flat with all mod cons. Each night Astrid and I would tart ourselves up, drive into the centre of Hamburg in Astrid's little car and arrive at the club just in time to hear the boys begin their night's stint. The very large stage was bare except for the boys, their amplifiers and instruments. The way they dressed appeared to be of little importance to them or their audience. All that was required of them was to play their music and set the club alight, which is precisely what they did. The drink and the pep pills were an integral part of the boys' night. They would play for an hour or two at a time non-stop; they would then have a 'powsa', which was a fifteen minute break. Without the drink and pills they would have been exhausted, for the performances lasted until the club closed at two o'clock in the morning. Astrid, Dot and myself would sit on a table near the stage, totally absorbed by their growing capabilities, and in the way that they handled themselves in the face of the audiences. The music had even the loudest of drunks silenced by its sheer force and volume. Their repartee with the crowd was brilliant, half in German half in English. The English was for their own benefit—a banter of mickey-taking and caustic wit aimed directly at some of the drunken fools of Germans who couldn't understand a word, but laughed along, unaware that the joke was on them. On one particular night John got more and more pissed. He fell about the stage in hysterical convulsions with so much booze and so many pills inside him that he was no way in control. He was still making sense with his guitar playing, which he could do in his sleep. That night ended with John sitting on the edge of the stage in a very unsteady manner with an ancient wooden toilet seat round his neck, his guitar in one hand, and a bottle of beer in the other completely out of his mind.

When the club closed we usually went across the road to grab a bite to eat. Although it was late and the boys had worked themselves almost to a frazzle, the pills and booze would still be having their effect. Spirits were high and they were all full of devilment. They would leap and shriek down the streets as though they had just been let out of prison, joking and fooling amongst themselves and usually ending up in an exhausted heap on the dirty Hamburg pavements, laughing so much that we were all in tears.

Tears of laughter were the only tears I shed on that

holiday. John and I spent as much time on our own as we could, which wasn't a great deal. Whenever there was a break we would slip upstairs to the communal bedroom to talk and make love. On one or two occasions, when John wanted me to stay with him instead of going home with Astrid, I slept with him in his single bottom-layer bunk-bed. Above us, twisting, turning and grunting in his sleep was George. The rest of them would be out for the count too, snoring or talking in their sleep. We found it very hard not to giggle or wake up these sleeping beauties. It was such a confined space and the smell of sweaty socks was less than sweet and the toilet facilities were virtually nil, so you can imagine I must have loved John a great deal.

5

Unrest and Reformation

Although everything was going well between John and myself at this time, Paul and Stuart were beginning to get on each other's nerves and were constantly bickering at each other. Paul picked on Stuart for his lack of talent and the fact that he wore sunglasses, in fact anything he could think of that would niggle Stuart. Stuart, being a very sensitive and peace-loving soul, restrained himself, but there were the odd occasions when it almost came to fisticuffs. It began as a confrontation of personalities, but Paul was really venting his own frustration because he was fed up playing rhythm guitar along with John. He wanted desperately to expand his musical ability by playing left-hand bass, which of course would leave Stuart out in the cold.

As it happened Stuart was beginning to hanker after his long-neglected painting. His own common sense told him that he was never going to be a great bass guitarist, and he was not the type of person to fool himself or anyone else in that respect. In any case Stuart's whole life had changed following his first meeting and subsequent love affair with Astrid. They really were like two peas in a pod. They dressed like twins, ate, slept, lived for each other. The very thought of going back to England without Astrid was ridiculous so the fifth Beatle quietly resigned before the proverbial bubble burst. Stuart decided to stay in Hamburg and live with Astrid in her mother's top flat. He enrolled in the local Art College with the promise ahead of a brilliant career as an artist. One Professor Eduardo

Paolozzi showed a great deal of interest in Stuart's paintings and his future looked very rosy. I was so happy for them and John was very relieved that everything had fallen into place without bad feeling on any side.

On my arrival back in Merseyside, my mother had some very exciting news which would affect us both in different ways. My cousin and her husband were emigrating to Canada and wondered if my mother would like to go with them to act as Nanny to their tiny baby, while they studied for their respective teaching careers. My mother was very dubious about the whole thing. How could she leave me? Where would I stay? How on earth could I cope on my own?

It didn't take me very long, though to convince her that she would be crazy to turn down such a fantastic opportunity. After all, I had just returned from a foreign country with such glowing reports. 'But where will you stay?' she asked. It was at this point that I had the answer which would solve all my problems. John's Aunt Mimi took in paying students; that would be perfect. I could lodge with Mimi and be close to John at the same time. What a great idea! Needless to say I hadn't even consulted John or Mimi, but I felt in my bones that there wouldn't be very much opposition to my idea. So it came to pass that Miss Powell moved in with all her worldly belongings to lodge with Mrs Mimi Smith, the afore-mentioned John Winston Lennon, and three male students of varying shapes and sizes. My mother, still feeling rather reticent about the whole set up, bid me a loving farewell and sailed off into the Canadian sunset. Our little terraced house in Trinity Road was rented out to a young married couple just expecting their first child and it was a long time before I was to visit Hoylake again.

Dot and I had gone on our trip to Hamburg during the Easter holidays. I moved in with John and Mimi at the beginning of the summer break, which meant I was very low on funds. My college grant for the previous year had virtually run out and the cheque for my last year at College was not due until the beginning of the Autumn term. I would have to earn some bread, find some holiday work to pay Mimi for my keep. When my Father was alive, and

I was at the Junior Art School, I had worked every Saturday at the local Woolworth store to earn pocket money. This had been my only experience of earning a living, apart from a holiday job in a guest house in Llandudno that Phyl and I took during our first year in college. John's home was in Woolton, and the closest shopping area was Penny Lane, a ten minute bus ride away. The largest store in the centre was a Woolworths, and as I had had some experience of Woolies, I toddled along armed with enthusiasm and a smile—not a reference in sight. Luckily Woolworths were always short of staff during the holiday period so I got a job on the cosmetics counter and for a short time it was great. The girls I worked with shared that marvellous Liverpool wit, as did the customers—lovely characters.

While all these changes were taking place, John returned to Hamburg once again after a short break in Liverpool. He was earning enough by this time to help Mimi out with the expenses, and at first everything was rosy. I worked happily at Woolworths and helped Mimi when I could with the housework. In fact I did try to fit in as a daughter rather than a lodger. Perhaps that was the trouble —two women loving the same man inevitably leads to jealousy somewhere along the line. I am not saying that anything unpleasant took place but I did find that John's love for me created an impossible situation with Mimi. My brilliant idea began to turn a little sour on me and the only solution was for me to move on. Where to move was the problem. My mother was on the other side of the world. My brother was living in Cheshire, but he had only been married for a short time and I had no desire to play gooseberry in that happy household. My last resort was Aunty Tess, who lived on the other side of Liverpool. I phoned and poured out my hard luck story to her and with a great deal of sympathy and understanding she said that I could move in with them as soon as I liked. For me that was the following day.

They came with their car, loaded it up with my belongings and off we went. I was begining to feel like a gypsy at a point in my life when stability was very necessary to my studies. As luck would have it, though, I passed my exams without too much trouble. The next big challenge in my life was teaching practice, which filled me with dread and horror. I was so self-conscious that the very thought of facing a class of children and actually trying to teach them something worthwhile gave me many a sleepless night. John's letters of love and encouragement were the only things that kept me going.

When teaching practice was allocated I was horrified to learn that I was to teach in a secondary school in Garston, twelve to sixteen year olds in one of the toughest areas in Liverpool. In addition, from my aunt's house I would have to take no less than three buses every morning to get to my destination. Student teachers are usually given a rough time in most schools and I just wanted to run away and hide. If the kids I was supposed to teach were anything like the Beatle fans from that area I was lost. I felt very lonely with John away in Hamburg and my mother in Canada. My aunt was a great friend to me but she couldn't avert my feelings of sheer panic. I was about to stand on my own two feet for the very first time and I didn't like it one bit. I think it couldn't have been worse if I had been condemned to the gallows than it was that first day.

As well as teaching older children we did further training in primary schools which really suited me. The children were so eager to learn, full of devilment but without the moodiness and problems brought about by puberty. In fact once I had overcome my initial fears of being thrown in off the deep end, as it were, I settled into my final year at college quite happily. Letters from John arrived with amazing regularity. 'Dear Cyn, Could you please send me the words to *A Shot Of Rhythm And Blues*. It won't take long.' I would dutifully go out and buy the record in question and spend hours driving everyone crazy with the record on 33⅓ rpm, playing it over and over again until I had all the words perfect. On occasions I would fall in love with certain records for their appropriately amorous lyrics and send them off to John with my replies, hoping that the message would sink in.

With all the travelling I was doing from my aunt's home to school and college, the expense and inconvenience was beginning to get me down. I decided to go completely independent and look for a bedsit closer to college. Dot and I scoured the Liverpool *Echo* in search of something cheap and suitable. It was all very exciting, a place of my own, and when I wrote to John relating my intentions, his reply was more than enthusiastic. At last we could be alone together and the vote in favour was unanimous.

My romantic, idealistic ideas of my future flat, however, were a very far cry from the room I eventually ended up in. It was reasonably close to college and all the schools I was training at and I suppose you could say it had all mod cons: hot and cold running rust in the bathroom; one shilling a time to heat the water for a bath of water which barely reached above the ankles; a single-bar electric fire; a minute one-ring cooker; a single bed and a moth-eaten chair and rug. There was a very strange inhabitant in the room next door, an elderly lady, a recluse who surrounded herself with cats, bags of coal and filth. She didn't appear to leave her room for the outside world, and she was an absolute pain in the neck as far as I was concerned. If I opened the door for anything at all she would be out on the landing nosing and poking into everything, borrowing shillings for the meter by the minute. I don't think the poor old girl had had a wash in years and the smell from her room nearly knocked you over as you passed en route to the front door.

Being young and full of enthusiasm, even the dirtiest of hovels would have been viewed by me through rose-coloured glasses. Out came the paint, disinfectant and pink light bulbs. I was going to make it beautiful for when John came home and that was all that mattered.

When John eventually did come home to my room it was under very tragic circumstances. Stuart had died of a brain tumour at the age of twenty-one. We all knew that poor Stuart had been suffering the most awful pain from frequent headaches. No one in the medical profession had been able to relieve him. He was literally going out of his mind with the agony, even to the extent of trying to throw himself out of the window of his flat. Poor Astrid had thankfully been there to drag him back. Stuart died in her loving arms in an ambulance on the way to a Hamburg hospital. A bright and beautiful flame extinguished so painfully and suddenly. I couldn't help thinking of their first meeting when Stuart arranged a rendezvous with Astrid clutching a single white rose to give to her. The language problem was so completely irrelevant. Theirs was a beautiful love so full of joy and yet so short lived. How cruel when they had everything to live for. Stuart was working on some of his finest canvasses prior to his untimely death and to my mind he would have been hailed as one of the great painters if he had lived and had the opportunity to really prove himself.

So it was with heavy hearts and shocked expressions that John and I met again. The boys still disbelieving the awful facts had returned home for Stuart's funeral. Astrid was a shadow of her former self, yet she was so wonderful. Her inner strength calmed us all down, yet she must have wanted to die herself at that time.

Although we were all in a real state of shock we knew we had to pull ourselves together and get on with the job of living and working. Sadly, the boys went back to Hamburg, knowing that it could never be the same again yet needing the work and money to survive. On this particular return journey they would be playing for a man called Manfred, who owned the very large Star Club, again in the Reeperbahn. They were being offered more money and the living quarters were positively luxurious in comparison to their previous digs. John wrote home to me with great excitement that they even had a shower all to themselves. So they could now be clean little rockers.

John, Paul and George were becoming closer knit in every sense. Their music was tight and together, improving by leaps and bounds, their personalities became increasingly in tune with each other. I don't remember any serious clashes occurring between them. The zany sense of humour that was a strong attraction with their fans was an integral part of each one of them, except Pete. As I have said he just wasn't on the same wavelength and it was beginning to irk the boys. They needed a really good drummer who could fit into their exclusive club, someone who would

68

entertain them as much as they entertained each other, on and off the stage.

During their stays in Hamburg, Astrid shot reel after reel of film of the boys. She loved them as subjects and it was she who was instrumental in changing their image. They didn't lose their endearing scruffy appeal or their character, but Astrid introduced a touch of class, in the shape of black leather trousers and casual bomber jackets. At Astrid's suggestion, they altered their hair styles into a softer greaseless shape which improved their whole appearance. From that moment the teddy boy era was on its way out and the Mop Tops were in. The photographs were mean and moody impressions in black and white. I think only Paul ever smiled, the diplomat as ever. John wouldn't do anything he didn't want to, but Paul even in those early days could have earned a living in public relations. He would work his back-side off in potentially explosive situations in order to keep things on an even keel, unless of course he was the instigator which was rare. George didn't come across as a very strong character. He was lean and hungry looking with a broad toothy grin, very quiet most of the time but dedicated to his music. He was happy just playing and fitting in with the whole set up and usually followed John's lead. John emerged as the leader whenever a leader was wanted. He wasn't elected, he just *was* without question.

Dot and I were becoming very close friends. The fact that the boys were away so much of the time threw us ever closer together. She would stay with me whenever possible as I found weekends very lonely stuck in a pokey room without company. My work and preparation for lessons did take up a great deal of my out of college hours but the social side of my life was abysmal without John. The thought of dating anyone else was out of the question, being a one man woman by nature. It was about three weeks after I had settled into my new way of life when the old girl in the next room left rather mysteriously. The room was vacant for quite a while which was rather unnerving until I had a brainwave. I would ask the landlady if I could move in and Dot could move into my old room.

It all worked out fine once Dot had convinced her parents that she wasn't going to be led astray. After all it was a big step for a young girl in those days and not at all the accepted thing as it is today. We had made our respective nests ready for the wanderers' return. John was over the moon. An extract from one of his letters reads, 'My voice has gone since I got here (it was gone before I came if I remember rightly) I can't seem to find it—ah well, I can't wait to see your new room. It will be great seeing it for the first time and having chips and all and a ciggie (don't let me come back to a regular smoker please, Miss Powell). Hmmm, I can just see you and Dot puffing away, I suppose that's the least of my worries. I miss, miss, miss you Miss Powell' . . . and so on.

When the stint in Hamburg finally came to an end the boys returned to Liverpool and were hailed as conquering heroes by their loyal fans. The now famous Cavern Club had previously made its name as a jazz club, but Liverpool rock groups had grown in popularity so much that the owner Ray McFall decided that it would be in his interest to take advantage of the rock boom. On their return the boys were booked to do some dates at the Cavern. Whilst in Hamburg the boys had made a record with Tony Sheridan for Bert Kaempfert. At the time it was a great experience and the excitement of all concerned was boundless, John, Paul, George and Pete were the backing group for Tony who had a really powerful voice. The record was *My Bonnie*. Little was heard of the record following our hopes of success until the Beatles hit Liverpool in a really big way.

The atmosphere in the Cavern was like nothing else on earth. It was situated in Mathew Street, a narrow cobbled back alley in the centre of Liverpool's thriving commercial area. An unimpressive street full of warehouses, lorries and litter. The Cavern was in the cellar of one of these warehouses. The entrance was tiny, the stairs leading into the dank depths of the cellar were narrow and uneven. The unsavoury aroma of damp and sweat pervaded even the most blocked up of nostrils, a common complaint in Liverpool.

The lunchtime sessions were a phenomenal success.

'Ah come on Pauly give us *Red Sails in the Sunset* for our Mary'

Young city ladies and gents, students, shop assistants, factory workers and school children would queue impatiently along the narrow pavement to obtain their daily fix of sounds, sounds of which they had never heard the like before. The cellar itself had three sections. The central section afforded rows of wooden cane seated chairs, the side areas were for the boppers; bench seats skirted the dripping walls. Each section was open plan, divided only by supporting walls and low brick archways, very solid in their construction. The lighting was almost non-existent except for the odd well-concealed red light bulb. A den of iniquity you might think? Not a bit of it. Once the music commenced, the crowd were as one. 'Electrifying' is the only word I can use to describe that atmosphere. The surrounding walls and arches seemed to fade away into infinity leaving only the mass of humanity, over-heated, screaming their appreciation to the point of blowing their fuses, swaying, clapping, heaving bodies caught up in the indescribable ecstasy of the explosion of their pent-up emotions. Water would drip from the ceiling and run down the walls and as the music got louder so would the screams —a truly incredible scene. The Beatles were number one in everyone's charts. They would grab their audience musically, emotionally and sexually, take them with them for the ride and when the trip was over would leave them totally exhausted yet screaming for more. I had never seen anything like it. It was fantastic. The stage of the Cavern was very small, enough room for a piano, amplifiers, microphones and drums. The compère Bob Wooler, a very competent and dedicated man, would introduce the various groups with great professionalism and style. In the early days he was very much out of his depth with the boys due to his tremendous self-discipline and views of what performers should and should not do on stage.

For Astrid

Please give her strength in her dark hour
Fire her with hope so she may tower
Above the depths of sad despair.
This day she feels no hope in sight

Please give her strength so she may fight
The fears that hold her in their grasp
Please give strength 'til all is past.
Life must go on yet some may leave
To give new life a chance to breathe.
A chance to learn as we have learned
Through times of sadness we have earned
A certain wisdom—yet more to come
We all will learn when life is done.

To Dorothy

I know we'll meet again some day,
How can I put in words and say
The pleasure you have given me.
The pleasure of your company.

You know as much as I, how much
I'll miss your presence, ever present
Are my thoughts of times so pleasant,
Words are not enough without the touch.

There's an empty place today,
an empty void, a missing friend,
An empty word no ear to bend.
Enjoy yourself is all I say,
Maybe we'll meet again some day.

6

Brian Epstein and Consolidation

It was at this point, as their reputation was growing in intensity, that Brian Epstein wandered into the Cavern full of curiosity, to observe the boys at first-hand. Brian's background was upper middle class and Jewish. His occupation, which he found very boring, was in the family business— furnishing and records. It was because of a request in his shop for the Beatles record *My Bonnie* that one lunch-time Brian found himself, totally out of character, standing at the back of the Cavern, heart beating fast, adrenaline zooming, completely overwhelmed by the sights and sounds that crashed into him. He found it all too much for him to resist. The idea of managing this dynamic quartet began to grow in his mind with alarming rapidity. He was ob-sessed and his obsession had to be satisfied.

When eventually Brian propositioned the boys with his ideas and promises of fame and fortune, he came up against very little resistance. Brian was just what they needed. He was beautifully dressed, very well spoken and, to the boys, the fact that his family owned a large business concern in the centre of Liverpool really impressed them. Although Brian had had no experience in the world of music and with record companies, he hankered for the bright lights of the entertainment field. He was a very dis-appointed, failed R.A.D.A. student but entertainment was still in his blood. He would make a name for himself even if it killed him, a sentiment that was to become reality. Be-fore the formality of cementing the arrangement with Brian, the boys' dissatisfaction with their line-up had to be ironed out. Pete was still with them, still giving them his all, but it was not enough. By pure coincidence Rory Storm's drummer Ringo Starr decided that he had had enough of England and had ideas of emigrating to America. He left the group and was in between a job and a new life. Little did he dream of what form his new life would take. The Beatles were now faced with a very delicate situation. They desperately wanted Ringo in and Pete out, before any binding contracts were signed. Whilst all this excitement on the professional side was going on, I was a very worried young lady indeed. Young girls nowadays have all the advantages of enlightened discussions about the then taboo subject of sex. But then the contraceptive pill was just a twinkle in some bright medic's eye. In my particular case it was more a matter of 'ignorance is bliss'. I was blinded by love and blind to the consequences. It couldn't happen to me, not now, not before I've had a chance of proving myself in some sort of profession, not before I'm married. God, what will my mother say? My monthly friend did not pay me a visit and I was distraught. I had already sunk to the depths, my money had run out and I had been forced to apply for social security (another stigma in those days). The very first time I visited the Social Security offices in Liverpool I bumped into an aunt of John's directly outside. My embarrassment was so obvious by my red face and stuttered greetings, no way could I reveal anything other than guilt. How silly it all seems now, but then it was a different matter as was finding oneself pregnant outside marriage. Morning sickness and the advice of a friend who was familiar with all the symptoms, drove me to Phyllis's doctor. Phyl came with me for support and I really valued her friendship and confidence then more than ever. I walked shakily into that lady doctor's surgery, hands trembling, voice almost inaudible with fear, praying to God that it would be all right, just a quirk of nature, anything other than the dreadful truth. Believing that a lady doctor would be sympathetic I sat down on the edge of the chair in front of her desk. Outside, I remember, the sun was shining and the world looked beautiful, to all but me. Once again my courage and self-control were being put to the test. Following my tearful outburst of condition and symptoms, she frostily, and disdainfully examined me. My worst fears were confirmed, I received no sympathy or understanding, just a high-handed, heartless lecture on behaviour and morals. I left that doctor's surgery believing that the end of the world was in view. My outlook had never been bleaker.

A few weeks before my earth-shattering discovery Dot was also to have her happy world turned upside down. On the night in question we were going about our business in our rooms as usual. Dot had just washed her hair and looked like something from outer space, with her hair in rollers and (God only knows why) she was dressed in a tatty old sweater and a pair of her mother's bloomers. Nobody was around to see the apparition so all was well and we'd had a few giggles about 'if they could only see us now'. We were both happy and relaxed when there was a knock on the door. The one and only Paul had arrived unexpectedly. Dot was absolutely horror-struck. There was nothing she could do about the way she looked. The pair of them rushed off into the privacy of Dot's room and all went very quiet. I was beginning to wonder if they were still alive when the door to Dot's room was opened and closed very quietly followed by the sound of footsteps speedily running down the stairs and the front door slamming fit to shake the foundations of the house. I was wondering what the hell was going on when Dot virtually collapsed into my room in hysterics. Crying and moaning like a wounded animal, her face blotchy, the so-carefully-applied rollers haphazardly falling out, strands of tear-wet hair in straggles round her crumpled little pixie face, and still wearing her mother's bloomers. Poor little defenceless Dot. She wouldn't harm a fly but had been hurt so much that she couldn't even tell me without renewed convulsions and outbursts of uncontrollable crying. As it happened she didn't need to tell me anything. Only one thing would have done that to Dot and that was Paul giving her the push. With the adulation of their fans came such a varied choice of submissive dolly-bird groupies willing to do *anything* for their new-found idols. A temptation Paul found hard to resist. After all he was a hot-blooded young rocker with a world full of beautiful women just waiting to be discovered by him. He was too young to settle down; he wanted desperately to be foot-loose and fancy-free and I suppose he let Dot down very gently under the circumstances. The trouble was that Dot honestly believed at the time that it was because of the way she looked on that fateful night.

Within a couple of days, once the reality of the situation had sunk in, Dot sadly collected her thoughts and her baggage together and went back home. I hardly saw Dot again. It was impossible, too close to home for her to bear. So another close friendship bit the dust. It seemed that this was to be a period of great change. Dot's sad exit, Brian's introduction, and my future production. My examinations were over, taken while I was half asleep as I had been up half the night with John, his long-awaited arrival home coinciding imperfectly with my finals. I knew I was fighting a losing battle.

But life still had its funny side. On one occasion before Dot left, John was caught well and truly with his pants down, or should I say his boots off, by my landlady. She was very irregular with her weekly rent collections; I never knew when to expect her. One Saturday morning John and I were snuggled up together, when we heard 'Yoo-hoo, it's only me,' mingling with our waking dreams. Realizing we weren't dreaming we both sat bolt upright. 'Jeez, what the hell do we do now?' John cursed and muttered. His clothes were in an untidy heap on the floor next to his big high-heeled winkle-picker boots. After running around half-naked in circles, with me in a state of panic screaming as quietly as I could that I would be thrown out on the street if she found out I had someone staying with me, I grabbed my dressing-gown, rushed like a bat out of hell into Dot's room, and left John to cope on his own, hoping that I could side-track her in some way. But I had forgotten all about the electricity meter that she had to empty. It was in my room close to the bed so there wasn't a thing I could do to help. She charged upstairs, straight into my room. My number was up or so I thought. Then there was a knock on the door of Dot's room and she broke in on a very tense atmosphere. To my surprise she beamed at

77

us both, gave us such a funny look, and didn't say a dicky bird—just collected the rent and waved us a breezy good-bye.

When we heard the front door close behind her Dot and I fell about laughing and giggling with relief forgetting all about John. We suddenly realized that everything was quiet next door, so in we crept to investigate. John's enormous boots were very much in evidence at the foot of the bed, but no sign of him anywhere until I called his name. The untidy mound of bedclothes suddenly erupted and flew in all directions. A very dishevelled and red-faced, breathless John appeared and let out a few choice words concerning his near-suffocation and 'Why didn't the bloody woman give us more warning?' The landlady must have had a great laugh at our expense.

All very funny, but now I had to let John know the results of my visit to the doctor. It wasn't easy, in fact it was heartbreaking for me to have to tell him under such circumstances. Even at that point I hadn't even considered marriage to John, it just wasn't a subject that was ever broached. Being together was all we wanted without contracts or marriage lines to hold us together. On only one occasion had John ever mentioned anything remotely connected with marriage. It was in one of his letters to me which coincided with Paul buying continental engagement rings for himself and Dot. John obviously liked the idea and suggested that it was about time we did something about getting engaged too, but nothing was ever done about it.

Circumstances now forced a decision upon us. Feeling very sick and faint, with all the fight knocked out of me, I broke the news to John. After tearfully blurting out the results of my examination by the doctor, I watched his face drain of all its colour, and fear and panic creep into his eyes. He was speechless for what seemed like an age. I stared at him, my heart pounding so fast I thought I would pass out. Finally John broke the interminable silence.

'There's only one thing for it, Cyn, we'll have to get married.'

There didn't seem to be any question in his mind about his decision as he had had a very conventional upbringing.

He knew 'right' from 'wrong'. And although I knew that neither of us were ready for marriage, let alone the responsibility of a baby I was so relieved. In my teens when most girls were preoccupied with marriages and babies, I had been too busy studying and growing up, especially after my father died. Babies, as far as I was concerned, were always dirty-nappied screaming bundles that took up a great deal of time and energy and belonged to somebody else, it hadn't even crossed my mind that one day I would produce one.

Once the truth was out in the open and the initial shock had been sustained by us both, John was in fear and dread of telling Mimi. In fact I think John found it easier accepting the fact than facing Mimi with it. He trundled off into the dark damp night with a great weight on his young shoulders, wishing I'm sure that he would wake up soon and find that it had been a bad dream.

John's confrontation with Mimi was not a pleasant one. He was very cagey about telling me exactly what happened, mainly because he didn't want to hurt my feelings. But what did come over loud and clear was the fact that Mimi was hurt and disgusted and that she wouldn't under any circumstances condone the affair by being present at the wedding. She would have nothing to do with it and neither would the rest of the family. So that was that. One down one to go.

It was wonderful to see my mother again after such a long time. She arrived bearing gifts of all shapes and sizes, and looked so well and so happy that I just couldn't spoil her holiday with my news. She took one look at my room and immediately paid a visit to her favourite sale-room, hired a van and arrived on my doorstep loaded up with carpets, curtains, everything she could lay her hands on that in her view would brighten the place up for me. But she wasn't to be here for long and I knew I would have to tell her. She was staying with my brother and his wife Margery at their home in Meols on the Wirral, so I invited myself for the last weekend of her stay. Heart in mouth and nerve ends visible I told her. It was her last night in England. My poor mother was speechless, but my fears of her having a fit melted away into the warmth of her understanding and love. Her only concern was for me and the fact that she couldn't possibly put off leaving the next day.

John had been acting very quickly during my absence. He had been to Brian for help and advice. Brian suggested a special licence which John obtained from Hope Street Registry Office. And the date had been set for the day after my mother's sailing back to Canada.

I was overcome with sadness when my mother left. I hadn't felt as bad since the death of my father. I felt as though I was never going to see her again. Seeing off someone you love is always difficult, even on the happiest of occasions. On this occasion I found it unbearable. I felt like a tiny child losing everything I held dear being plunged into an abyss of doubt and uncertainty, even though it was to be with the man I loved. I managed a smile and choked back the tears for my mother's sake as she boarded and sorted herself out for the long sea voyage. As soon as all visitors were requested to disembark, I hugged her to me and the contact opened the flood-gates. After kissing her goodbye I rushed down the gangway trying to lose myself amidst the crowds of waving smiling people, hands covering my wet, miserable face. All my pent-up fears and emotions exploded and with Tony's and Margery's comforting arms around me I was led weeping to the quay-side to wave my last goodbyes. I couldn't even see who I was waving to, my eyes were so blurred and puffy with tears.

And so it was on August 23rd, 1963, that John Winston Lennon and Cynthia Powell were joined in holy matrimony. It was a wedding to end all weddings. Something old, something new. Something borrowed. Something blue. I had plenty of the old; was feeling very blue; and had a very new life growing inside me! Brian lent us his car to ferry me to the ceremony so I suppose you could say I had all the requirements for a happy bride. The old I mention were my clothes. My wedding outfit consisted of a well-worn purple and black check two-piece suit, a white, frilly high-necked blouse (which Astrid had given to me), black shoes and hand-bag—not exactly the vogue wedding outfit of the year! But I put my hair up very tidily in a french pleat and was feeling quite smart and full of excitement by the time Brian picked me up on that fateful day. It was a very dull morning; the sky was overcast and grey, threatening heavy rain. Brian looked very dapper in his pinstriped ensemble and the sight of him filled me with a new confidence. To cap it all, Brian offered us his very nice flat in Faulkener Street, just around the corner from the Art College, which he hardly ever used. It was furnished and ready for immediate occupation. I was over the moon. What a wedding gift! Brian was embarrassed by my show of emotion. John and I hadn't even thought about where we were going to live after the wedding, being so overwhelmed by what was happening at the moment. It was a God-send.

Those present at the wedding included my brother Tony and his wife, Paul and George, Brian and, not forgetting the man himself, John. The scene that greeted me on my arrival was hysterically funny. It was more like a funeral than a wedding. John, George and Paul huddled together in one corner of the drably decorated waiting room. All of them wore black suits, white shirts and black ties. Their faces were pale and strained, their hands fidgeted nervously, alternately adjusting their ties and loosening their collars, or running their hands through their well combed hair—almost in unison! Nervous whisperings could be heard and the occasional stifled giggle threatened everyone's self-control. Tony and Margery appeared totally bemused by the whole situation. Doubtless Tony's worried and puzzled expression revealed his fears for the future of his little sister. This was definitely not *his* idea of how a marriage should be. John's family stuck to their decision to boycott the occasion—a sad statement of their lack of understanding. Needless to say my mother's absence upset me although I had so much on my mind I had little time to reflect on what might have been.

Following the usual hugs and kisses of greetings outside we waited with bated breath for the door of the Registry Office to open. Eventually we were welcomed into the sanctified room by a man as dreary looking as the day itself. I think one look at us must have put him in a bad mood for the rest of the day. He obviously took his job very seriously. So seriously that he had forgotten how to smile. Indeed the solemnity of the occasion caused us all to bow our heads, the silence was overpowering, broken only by the Registrar's low key instructions and questions. My legs turned to jelly in anticipation of the service; my throat was drying up; fears of not being able to answer his questions tightened my throat even more. Brian was best man; Tony and Margery the witnesses.

We were ready to begin. John and I looked straight ahead out of the window, a view totally obscured by high brick walls. And in the backyard of the adjoining building was a cloth-capped workman firmly grasping in his dirty calloused hands a pneumatic drill. As if he knew it were his cue, the moment the ceremony commenced he began drilling. None of us heard a word of the service; we couldn't even hear ourselves think. The beauty of the words and the importance of the vows we were making were drowned by the cacophony of sounds created by rattling windows and ear-splitting drilling which might as well have been in the room with us. Trying to keep straight faces and our minds on the enormity of the step we were taking was an impossibility. All we wanted to do was get out, get it over with as soon as possible; release the tension of the claustrophobic confines of what seemed to us at the time a madhouse. It was all totally unreal.

When finally we emerged from the portals of the Registry Office, reality hit us. Despite everything we were all very much aware of what those chaotic moments meant to us and our future. I was now Mrs Cynthia Lennon. John had not only gained a headache, he had gained a *wife* and the promise of a child in only eight months—possibly a bigger headache. Perhaps, appropriately, the moment we stepped out into the streets of Liverpool, the heavens opened. Torrential rain cascaded onto the pavements and ran into the gutter to join the ever-increasing rivers of dirty water that sped down the hill. It was so romantic! Old newspapers and sweet wrappers bobbed and danced their merry way down the channels of fast-running water. But for this at least I was prepared, I had an umbrella. This bride was not going to get wet!

Our wedding reception was really something. Reeces Café! Tony and Margery bade us farewell, kisses for all

'Do you take this pneumatic drill'

under a dripping brolly, passers-by shoving and pushing to get past, hurrying to avoid the rain and hungry for their lunches—totally unaware that such an important event had just taken place. Tony had to get back to work, so the remainder of the happy little band waved goodbye and rushed off to the reception. Hungry, wet and elated by this time we entered Reeces for our lunch. Lunchtime Reeces is always crowded and that day was no exception, not a seat to be had unless of course we waited. I was beginning to think that the gods were against us when a table became vacant. We rushed over to it with great lack of finesse and sat down with sighs of relief. The menu was a run-of-the-mill set luncheon. Soup, roast chicken and trifle—a veritable feast. I think the toast to the happy couple was with water as Reeces weren't licensed. So that was our wedding day in all its glory and quite honestly it beat all the church weddings that I had ever been to as a truly memorable occasion. What's more it only cost us fifteen shillings. Brian paid for the lunch.

It took us only a short time to settle into Brian's flat. It was beautifully furnished in comparison with my old digs and our personal belongings were few and far between. The flat extended the full length of the ground floor and we even had the luxury of a small, walled garden. The only snag was that our bedroom was situated at the front of the house overlooking Faulkener Street. Access to the rest of the flat was only by going through the main hall and past the front door which was used by all the other tenants of the house—very inconvenient when in need of the bathroom during the night. Anyone could wander in through the front door and walk from the street into our rooms if the door was left open and although the house itself was a beautiful old terraced property, the neighbourhood was very salubrious. It all made me very nervous at times, especially when John was away on tour. On one terrifying occasion I had retired to bed, John had locked up and was just about to get undressed, when the front door bell rang. Hoping that someone else would answer, we ignored it for a while. Then the ringing became more urgent and it was obvious that we would have to go and investigate. Both a little nervous due to the fact that it was about midnight, John opened the door only to be confronted by two really rough looking characters.

'Oh, hello skin!' the spokesman muttered in a very thick Liverpool accent. 'We were wondering, me and my mate here, if Carol's there.'

John feeling very uneasy about the situation replied hurriedly, 'Sorry, mate, I think you must have made a mistake, no one of that name lives here.'

Although it was obvious that they were not satisfied they muttered their thanks and appeared to leave. John reappeared in our bedroom after closing the vestibule door (the outside door was left open for the other tenants). All went quiet for a while until the pair of us fell out of bed with shock. Our door was being battered on with great force, the noise and the threat of violence behind the aggression was fearsome. John and I immediately clung to each other like frightened children.

'What the bloody hell is going on?' yelled John as the colour drained from his face. I grabbed the bedclothes and pulled them up to my chin.

'What do they want, John, they must be mad, what are we going to do?' I cried in real fear.

'We're bloody trapped, aren't we? If only I could get into the other room at least I could get a knife and defend us. Bloody hell what are they after. They must be bloody lunatics.'

Whilst our fears were increasing by the second, the banging and noises of metal objects being forced into the lock seemed to be increasing too. Above the noise came threatening shouts from thugs. 'We know she's there, you dirty ponce. We'll bloody tear you apart when we get our hands on you. You bloody hand her over or else!'

It was at this point that I couldn't take it any more, I finally found my voice and with all the courage and strength I could muster I shrieked in desperation so the whole Street could hear. 'The only bloody woman in this bloody room is me and my name is not Carol, it's Cynthia, and for your information I'm three months pregnant.' After I had done my bit for survival I collapsed in a heap on the bed shaking like a leaf, only then realizing that all had gone silent. It was unbelievable. The conversation behind the door became muttered and inaudible. We heard their shuffling footsteps fade and the front door close. John and I took a long time getting to sleep that particular night!

Finally Brian signed up the Beatles *including* Ringo. He set out with all the enthusiasm and determination in him to win a recording contract. Toting their tapes around every recording company in London he tried to convince the record moguls of the great talents of his boys. He found it very hard going and was turned down so many times that he was beginning to give up hope, when George Martin, from E.M.I., listened and liked what he heard. They were signed up by E.M.I. and their first record was to be their own composition. The magic combination of group and doting manager was about to be let loose on the unsuspecting public. We were all overjoyed to put it lightly. Everything seemed to be coming up roses at last. Due to all the successful business dealings in London the boys were required to spend a great deal of their time travelling backwards and forwards to the big City. I found myself more and more on my own. When I did see John it was usually for very short periods and most of that time was spent washing and ironing his entire wardrobe ready for his next trip. It was on one of John's 'home' days that I was first introduced to Ringo. He was totally unaware of the fact that we were married or that I was 'in the club'. As we said our hellos I had the distinct feeling that I was being viewed with great suspicion, in fact we were very wary of each other for quite a while. I wondered at the time if it was because of the old 'over the water' syndrome.

Loneliness continued to spread over me and it was during one of John's three-day trips to London that I had the shock of my life. I was losing blood. Panic sent me rushing off to the doctor with Phyl, frightened and unhappy at the prospect of losing my child after all we'd been through. The doctor's diagnosis was very depressing. 'There is always the danger of miscarriage during the first pregnancy, and I'm afraid if you don't go home and get into bed immediately there is every possibility that you may lose your child.' The journey back to the flat was worrying. The bus seemed to go over every bump and pothole in the road and I was convinced I wouldn't make it. I walked in slow motion, Phyl held on to me trying to comfort and encourage me. Eventually when I climbed into bed and Phyl left to go back to work it finally got home to me that I was totally alone. I phoned my brother, but he had to work as did Margery. There was no one I could turn to. The thought of having a miscarriage in such isolation filled me with fear and dread. I spent three very miserable lonely days in bed, the bathroom was too far for me to manage so a bucket by the bed and a kettle were my only facilities. I just lay there reading and thinking, hoping and praying that all would be well. Luckily I had gone to the doctor just in time and my unborn child was not going to be disposed of that easily. We both survived, much to John's relief on his return.

Ironic as it turned out, my situation was soon to be altered for the better. It was on a beautiful sunny, crisp Autumn afternoon that John and I decided to go out. Where? We weren't sure until I suggested we pay Mimi a visit. There is one thing that really upsets me and that is bad blood created by unnecessary rifts. Although John's mother wasn't alive and his father didn't figure in his life any more the importance of good relationships within his existing family was crucial in my eyes. So I persuaded him to forget all the hurt and make it up with them.

Mimi welcomed us with open arms. She was so overjoyed to see John again. In fact we were all overwhelmed by the reunion. After a welcome meal we sat and talked non-stop.

'Cynthia, I'm very worried about you,' Mimi said. 'You shouldn't be stuck in that flat in the back-of-beyond without some one to look after you while you're pregnant.'

I had to agree with her on this point. I wasn't very happy or sure of myself where we were, I was lonely and at times very nervous. It hadn't been a very lucky place. Mimi went on to suggest that we move back in with her. We could have the ground floor of the house and she would move upstairs and make it self-contained. It all sounded wonderful. We agreed and accepted her offer. The only snag for the time being was that we would have to muck in with the students until the Christmas holidays.

Just before we moved in with Mimi the record company released their first record *Love Me Do*. The Beatles were beginning to gain a foothold in the British charts. Brian was ecstatic. A one-night stand tour of Britain with Helen Shapiro was organized. All the breaks were going our way and it was a breath-taking time. Everything had a dream-like quality about it. From the Jacaranda to stardom in next to no time—a marriage, a child and a future that looked very promising for all of us.

While the boys were becoming more and more of an ob-session with the British record buying public, I had been very delicately advised that it would be wise to keep a very low profile. It would be to everyone's advantage if the marriage of one of the Beatles was kept a secret. I must admit I didn't relish the thought of publicity. I was quite happy just getting on with the job in hand. I didn't even object to walking around without a wedding ring, but I did find it increasingly difficult trying to conceal my three-month large lump in the presence of the male students who were staying with Mimi. I had to be well-camouflaged all the time. Billowing blouses and over-large waistcoats were an essential part of my wardrobe. My hair too was proving a very difficult task for different reasons. Bleaching it myself was becoming increasingly awkward so I decided to go mad and have it done properly at one of the best hair-dressers in Liverpool. John was due home the next day so I thought I would make myself beautiful for his return. My hair was very long at the time and not being used to hairdressers and their love of getting hold of a head of long hair, I couldn't resist their insistence on using the scissors. I emerged shorn and in tears. My hair was my crowning glory and John wouldn't be seen dead with any-one with short hair. I rushed home feeling like the first lamb of the year to be shorn. The night *Please Please Me*, the Beatles' second record, hit the charts saw me feeling far from elated. I could only think of John's reaction to the new me. John arrived home very late that night and I was already in bed with my hair in rollers desperately try-ing to make something out of the disaster. The loving reunion was followed the next day by the unveiling. By John's expression, one would have thought I had turned green overnight. He was furious with me and he looked at me with such hate and anger I felt as though I had committed the basest of crimes. Incredible as it sounds he didn't speak to me for two whole days. He couldn't even bring himself to look at me. I was beginning to think that this was the end, and what a way to go, when John relented, realizing the stupidity of his irrational behaviour.

Please Please Me was a Number One hit, a phenomenal success. The Beatles were on the crest of a wave. They shook the very foundations of the music industry. Agents and publishers were clamouring for a part of the action, and Brian was counting his blessings and the profits with glee. His faith in the boys and his efforts were coming to fruition. A very sincere and conscientious man, he loved the Beatles dearly. They were his children, his family, his whole life. Whatever he did, he did for them. The opportunity for fulfilling all his ambitions was being presented to him in the shape of four scruffy lads from Liverpool. And his innate business sense told Brian that the scruff would have to go. Collarless beige suits were to take their place, uniformity in dress and hair-styles would present the clean-cut innocent image that would appeal to the public. 'Bloody hell, Brian, do we have to?' was the unanimous cry from the heart. 'I hate suits, Brian. We'll all look like a bunch of pansies.' 'They'll all think we're trying to copy the *Shadows*, Brian. Oh Christ, do we have to?' and so on. Brian was adamant. Publicity photographs were taken of the four, fresh-faced young innocents, grinning with embarrassment. It must have been embarrassing for John to grin! The mean and moody was out and the wholesome boy-next-door image was fast taking over, much against the grain with all of them. Professionalism was the name of the game and the stakes were high.

The winter of 1962–63 was the worst for years. Snow fell in abundance early on in the winter months and the freezing conditions turned the snow into hard-packed, treacherous ice, three-quarters of an inch deep. I had a wonderful pregnancy, following my early problems. I was healthy and content. John was whizzing around all over the country, success following success. Hysteria and Beatlemania was growing out of all proportion, but I was sheltered by the anonymity of my situation. Right now I was on the fringe of the madness, and it suited me very nicely. I was carried along by the thrill of their success, a dream was coming true. Twice a week I would visit doctor and hospital; each journey meant changing buses twice. I would slip and slide my way precariously to the bus stop in freezing fog, protecting the ever-growing lump from damaging falls and hoping and praying that I wouldn't be recognized. The hospital examinations were the most nerve-wracking. All the pregnant mums would be crammed together in the waiting-room and one by one our names would be called out. When mine came up I would be blowing my nose or tying a shoelace—anything rather than be recognised by an astute and discerning Beatle fan.

Over the Christmas period John and the boys were on tour again this time with Chris Montez and Tommy Roe. It was another huge success. Ringo fitted into their group like a dream. At last they had the perfect combination of talent. John and Paul were writing their songs with incredible ease and a speed which delighted Dick James, their fortunate music publisher. Winter flew by. The students moved out. Mimi moved upstairs and the date of the birth was upon me almost before I had time to think.

I was shopping in Penny Lane with Phyllis when the pains began. 'Oh my God,' I thought, 'this is it.' John of course was out on the road and there was no way I could contact him. So good old Phyllis offered to stay with me until the bitter end, and it was a bitter end for Phyl. In the middle of the night I let out a great yell, that was it, we phoned for an ambulance and in our nighties, slippers and dressing-gowns (and in Phyllis's case curlers) we were transported with incredible speed and efficiency to the Sefton General Hospital. On arrival I barely had time to bid Phyllis farewell before I was wheeled off down the corridors of the hospital. I was in safe hands which is more than could be said for poor friend Phyl. Dressed as I described, she was off-handedly informed that she was not to be transported back home by ambulance. She would have to make her own way home. The picture of her wandering the blackened streets of Liverpool in the freezing cold clad only in the flimsiest of night wear, hair in curlers, silly little feminine slippers on her feet and not a penny in her pockets fills me with horror every time I think about it. When Phyl told me the story herself it was hysterical. She said she was petrified. She had walked about two miles when a taxi came into view. Frantically she jumped up and down waving and shouting for him to stop. The poor man must have thought she had escaped from a mental home. Through sheer amazement he stopped. Trying to explain her predicament only made things worse. The first thing he said to her was, 'Hey, love, I don't think it's advisable to walk round the streets of Liverpool at this time of night dressed like that, do you?' Phyl didn't care what he thought of her by this time. He had agreed to take her home and that was all that mattered.

As I was wheeled off into the maternity wards, I was full of relief. At least I hadn't given birth to my offspring at home or on the way to the hospital. I hadn't inconvenienced anyone. I knew that I would be well looked after. I really thought that I would be in and out like a shot. Little did I imagine what I was in for. I was settled into one of the beds in a ward full of women, a third of whom had already done their bit. They sat up in their beds all shiny faced and proud of themselves. The rest of us poor mortals just about managed forced grins and infrequent snatches of conversations between bouts of pain from the labour contractions. White-clad nurses and doctors buzzed in and out of the wards like flies brandishing strange looking instruments which they prodded one's tender stomach with at hourly intervals. The girl in the next bed was enormous. She was a very big girl to begin with but with her additional mountainous lump she was gigantic. The poor unfortunate girl told me that she was unmarried and was very unhappy about the whole schmozzle. She also arrived the same time as myself so we watched each other's progress like hawks. As it happened neither of our babies were in any hurry to arrive. At first we tried to be very ladylike about the whole situation, but it proved impossible when we were into our second day of labour without producing anything more than louder groans and even louder grunts. Being on our own wasn't too bad, but when it came to visiting time the happy husbands would stream into the ward grasping bunches of flowers and chocolates for their even happier wives. The agony we went through was incredible as we tried not to upset these poor men with our screams. Every now and again the girl next to me would give up the struggle and in panic and sheer desperation would shriek out 'Mother . . . MOTHER . . . I want my Mother.'

Thankfully the doctor in charge also realized it was time for us to go, our strength was ebbing very fast and we now found ourselves in the labour room itself. Two beds surrounded by all sorts of weird and wonderful apparatus. We were both shown how to use the gas and air machine and were then left once more to our own devices. But it wasn't very long before my companion decided that she had just about had enough of all this pain and misery. In my drugged weak state I could hear her pleading cries for her mother which were increasing in their volume and regularity. The next utterance really amazed me. She yelled with great determination, 'I don't know about you but I can't stand any more of this. I'm going *home*.' And with that she pushed back the bedclothes and all I could see through the haze was a massive lumbering shape fly past me with incredible speed, hair and dressing-gown flying in her wake. She was off. I didn't see her again because the shock of it all seemed to have a magic effect. It set off the chain reaction of events for my own baby's birth. I was at last in labour proper.

At first all seemed to be going well but I was really too weak to do all that was required of me, I was just about to give up when a midwife warned me in no uncertain terms that if I didn't get up off my ass and push I'd have a dead baby on my hands.

That warning put the fear of God into me but had the desired effect. Julian was born at 7.45 a.m. on the Monday morning. It had been a very long weekend but it was well worth it. He was beautiful. The reason for the difficulty during Julian's birth was because the umbilical cord was wrapped around his neck, he arrived into this world an awful yellow colour, apart from that he was perfect, just perfect. It was two days before I could hold my baby in my arms and a week before I saw my husband.

'Ye owl 'ooo ah . . . mother! I want my mother'

John had been phoning Mimi nightly for progress reports on his wife and baby to be. On learning that he was the father of a healthy son, he was overjoyed yet unhappy that he couldn't see us both sooner. I had inquired if I could have a private room, knowing full well that we wouldn't have a minute's peace in the public ward (the cat would well and truly be out of the bag). So for the incredibly low price of twenty-five shillings a day, I had my own little room. Although the room was private it did look out onto the hospital corridors through large glass partitions. John's excited arrival however did not go unnoticed, he rushed through the door like a hurricane sweeping everything before him. It was a wonderful moment. 'Oh, Cyn, I love you, where is he then, who's a clever little Miss Powell then. Was it awful? Who does he look like?' I just couldn't get a word in edgeways, he was consumed with happiness and awe. When he eventually plucked up enough courage to pick the little bundle up he was full of pride and emotion. 'He's bloody marvellous, Cyn, isn't he absolutely fantastic . . . ? Who's going to be a famous little rocker like his Dad then?' Whilst this beautiful reunion was taking place, grinning faces were pressing themselves against the glass pane of the partition, groups of nurses and patients were gathering in the corridors, eager to gain a glimpse of a Liverpool celebrity. It started to get noisy, claustrophobic and very embarrassing, like being in a goldfish bowl. This incident was my first glimpse of how my life was to change drastically and it really unnerved me. Very quickly John became jumpy and on edge. He was beginning to feel trapped and it was time for him to escape but before he left he told me that Brian had asked him to go on holiday to Spain with him and he wanted to know if I objected. I must admit the request hit me like a bolt out of the blue and I really didn't take it in properly at first but when it sank in I suppressed my true feelings and acquiesced. I was well aware that John deserved a holiday. He had just completed a tour and recording sessions. In actual fact he had never really had a holiday as such. They had all been working very hard and under great pressure since the success of *Please Please Me,* so I concealed my hurt and envy and gave him my blessings. He was de-

94

lighted and left me a happy man. I on the other hand was left holding the baby, and what a baby.

As soon as John returned from his break in Spain, fully relaxed and raring to get going again, we went together to register our son's birth. We named him John, after his father, Charles after my father, and Julian the nearest we could get to John's mother Julia. Well pleased with his newly named son and accepting his newfound status as father with great pride John left home again for yet another tour, this time supporting a very big name, Roy Orbison. They really were making it big, their records were selling like hot cakes. Wherever one went people would be whistling or singing their songs, extolling their virtues, praising the new sound that was taking the country by storm. I, on the other hand, was the little woman at home trying desperately hard to cope single-handed with a baby that cried incessantly (he *was* a dreadful child in that respect). I ended up a nervous wreck trying to keep him quiet, knowing that Mimi wouldn't be having a minute's peace. I used to wrap him up well and push his pram to the very end of the garden and let him scream when I had done everything possible for him and hope and pray that he would tire himself out so that I could catch up on my sleep. In the end I was so exhausted that I was seeing double and all the feeling would go out of my arms and legs. John was really onto a good thing, being absent from all the joys of fatherhood in those early stages.

It was all very well, thinking back now, because when he did come home he would leave the room whenever I changed a nappy. He said that if he had stayed he would have been sick, and if he had had to put up with the crying night after night I'm sure he would have left home. My anonymity it appeared was still holding out. It really was amazing that the press hadn't sniffed me out. The local kids weren't so dumb though. I would be happily trotting along to the shops with my pride and joy in the pram when young girls would tap me on the shoulder and ask me if I was John Lennon's wife to which I would reply, 'John Lennon? Who's John Lennon? I've never heard of him. I think you must be mistaken. My name's Mackenzie,

I'm awfully sorry.' I would hurry off as quickly as my legs
would take me.

> The truth for me does not agree
> With other people using me
> With a freedom that they think is free.
> Checkmate will only find success
> When pawns themselves don't fall from grace.
> When honesty comes face to face
> With truth and not commodity.

> To use another's soul for gain,
> Misunderstanding all in vain,
> For those who use another's brain,
> To lift themselves with words profane.
> Cynics born to eat the words,
> Of men who falter not with swords.

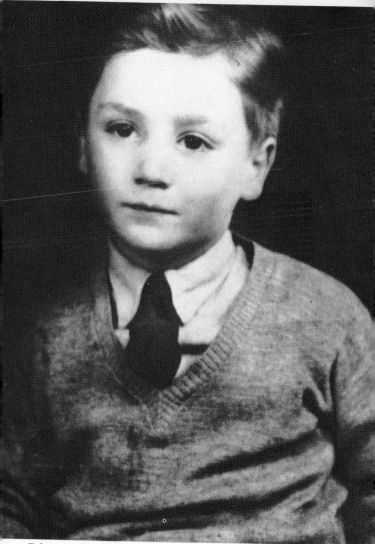

Primary school John.

John, Paul and the Quarrymen skiffle group.

Candid snap of John and mother mine in garden of Woolton home.

John and I on our way to America (First tour.)

Smiles and gladrags at the premiere of *Help*.

Living it up on an afternoon in Miami.

Relaxing after living it up in Miami.

Ringo entertains with an impromptu dance of joy.

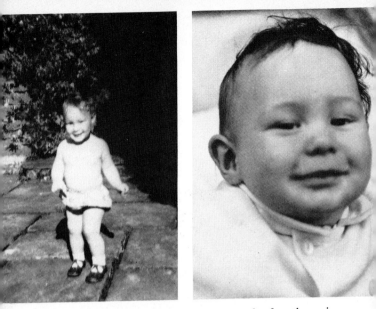

Above left: Sunshine and Julian in the grounds of our home in Weybridge. Above right: The first press photograph of Julian taken without our knowledge. Below: John, Julian and balloon.

Setting off for our visit to India and the Maharishi.

Premiere of *How I Won The War*.

John and director Dick Lester during the shooting of *How I Won The War*.

7

London Beckons

By the time Julian was six months old my mother returned home. She'd had her fill of Canada and was looking forward so much to seeing her first grandchild. Mimi by this time hated having to live in the upstairs of her own home; the hints were flying left, right and centre. I felt the old atmosphere rearing its ugly head again, so I decided to leave. John said he would be happy if I was. It didn't affect him very much as he was away so much of the time. I told him that it was absolutely ridiculous my being stuck in Liverpool for most of the time on my own and him in London working. It seemed to make sense to me that we made our base in London where everything appeared to be happening. John agreed and promised he would look for a place for us. So until John could find a place of our own my mother and I returned to Trinity Road, Hoylake. So much had changed since I left.

Before moving into Trinity, however, due to the fact that it still had a month's lease to go, Mum and I took a bedsit in Hoylake. My God we laughed and cried in that place. It was a large old house and all the other tenants were either retired, invalids, spinsters or creaky old bachelors. You can imagine the pair of us trying to control a self-willed belligerent baby in the communal kitchen and garden. We spent our days walking for miles with the pram, topping Julian's dummy up with rose-hip syrup and in the confines of our room virtually standing on our heads to amuse the little despot. All the time we had to remind ourselves laughingly of the predicament we were in compared with the fact that my husband was fast becoming a very wealthy man. Here we were in a five-pound-a-week bedsit with John Lennon's son and heir, absolutely non-existent as far as the rest of the world was concerned. We eventually moved back into our old home and sanity reigned for a while. Julian settled in beautifully. He even began to sleep like a normal child. John decided we should have a belated honeymoon when he returned home again and I was on cloud nine. Paris was to be our destination and at last we could have some time together again. It had been so long and I had missed him dreadfully.

Our journey to Paris was less than romantic, however, I was so excited that I worked myself up into such a state that on the morning of the flight I was as sick as a dog. I wouldn't give in though. I was determined it wasn't going to stop holiday plans, so off we went in a taxi. I was so ill. I lost count of the times the driver had to stop. We almost missed our flight due to me throwing up on the tarmac. I was such a mess, all because I was so happy and excited. When finally we descended onto the runway in France I felt fine. Paris was ready and waiting for us and we were eager to experience her. I was so happy in the knowledge that Julian was being well cared for by one of John's aunts and we were to be alone together for a whole week.

Our hotel in Paris was the George Cinque. Its opulence and style held us both in awe; it was the most expensive hotel in Paris. I had never before experienced such luxury and class. We both felt as though everyone was observing us with disdain and tittering between themselves, 'Darling, just look what the cat's brought in', or 'Look closely, darling, they have still got straw behind their ears.' We felt totally out of our depth but it didn't bother us too much. At least we could pay our bills and maybe even buy and sell some of them. Anyway we had each other. Our room was beautiful; the view from our window breath-taking. The bathroom was enormous. White marble from floor to ceiling. It was the first time I had ever seen a bidet. John had previously sent me a photograph of himself and Paul washing their feet in one. What a marvellous world we were living in and how lucky I was. One minute queueing up for Social Security in Liverpool, the next the George

'Bedtime in Paris'

99

Cinque, Paris, tomorrow the world. John and I were like two little kids. We did the tourist bit with relish—the Eiffel Tower, Montmartre, Le Arc de Triomphe. John had a movie camera with him and got up to all sorts of crazy antics. I bought a white beret and French perfume. It was wonderful; we were really living.

Following a particularly exhausting day of sightseeing John and I returned to our hotel shattered. With our key, the receptionist handed us a note; it was from Astrid. Somehow she had heard we were in Paris and by a wonderful coincidence so was she. Astrid was in Paris for only a few days holiday with a girlfriend and she would love to see us. Her phone number was printed at the bottom of the note so we hurried to our room and phoned.

That phone call led to the wildest night of our holiday. It was a night of true revelry—a French version of an English pub-crawl. The drink, rough red wine, was drunk with great gusto in all the bars of interest connected with the Artists' quarter of Paris, the more salubrious the better. As dawn broke over the roof tops we were still going great guns in a bar in the meat market surrounded by the market traders dressed in white bloodstained overalls. The air was thick with the smell of strong French cigarettes and we were absolutely blotto. After Hamburg we were really getting a taste for the hard stuff. Following a drunken almost inaudible unanimous decision that we'd had enough we stumbled and swayed our way to Astrid's lodgings for coffee. After crawling on all fours up a dark narrow staircase we collapsed in a heap at the top of the stairs. Shrieking with drunken hysteria we finally managed to get the key in the door and entered a room of minute proportions, very bohemian in its décor. Sprawled on the floor we drank our coffee *and* opened yet another bottle of plonk. When the last drop had been devoured John and I were paralytic —no way could we return to the George Cinque in that state. We couldn't even have hailed a taxi without falling over so it was decided that we stay with Astrid and her mate until we had slept it off. The only bed in the room was a single and believe it or not we all piled in and slept together like sardines. I would think that most men wouldn't have believed their luck under those conditions but John was in such a drunken stupor that nobody's virtue was in danger!

Following our fabulous holiday we returned to Hoylake and John was off again. I began to settle down again to the hum-drum day-to-day existence without him. He promised that he would find a place for us to live on this trip so I had that to look forward to.

All was very quiet on the western front until all hell let loose—hell in the shape of 'gentlemen of the press', At long last the cat was out of the bag concerning John's marital status and his child. The phone rang incessantly; my mother and I were besieged. A car was parked permanently outside the front door. Reporters and photographers seemed to appear from out of the woodwork. My mother did everything she possibly could to put them off the scent. I remember one particular occasion when she tried to pour cold water on their enthusiasm . . . 'Yes, I am Mrs Powell, no I'm afraid you must have made a terrible mistake. My daughter Cynthia does not live here and surely I would be the first to know if she was married and had a child. John Lennon? Oh yes, you mean one of those Beatle fellows. I think you must be having me on by suggesting any sort of relationship between my daughter and him; sorry I can't help you.'

Whilst all this confusion and subterfuge was going on I slipped out the back with Julian in his pram hoping to foil them while my mother held the fort. I walked hurriedly along the main market street in the hope that by the time I returned all would have cooled off. The only problem was that I was being kerb-crawled and photographed all the time with a telephoto lens camera. Too late I spotted it and rushed into a local greengrocer for refuge telling the owners about the situation I was in. They were so kind and accommodating and bundled the pair of us into the store-room of the shop just in time for me to avoid a confrontation with an eager reporter who had followed me hot-foot into the shop. The reporter's questions were twisted and turned back on him by my protectors. The man said that he knew I was there and only wanted a few words with me and then he would leave me in peace. To which my friends replied.

'I think you are very much mistaken. You must have seen her twin sister, she often comes here to do her shopping.'

I managed to avoid any confrontation with the press and I was feeling very pleased with myself until the following day when the news and photographs were splashed all over the front pages of the daily newspapers. John Lennon's 'secret' marriage was out and there was nothing anyone could do about it.

The undercover existence I had been living for such a long time was now over and I was happy and relieved. The play acting could be dispensed with and I could live like a normal human being again. On John's next visit to London he took me with him. He had become friendly with a chap called Bob Freeman and his wife. Bob was a photographer and was working on the Beatles' albums. When we paid them a visit we mentioned that we were looking out for a flat and Bob helped us a great deal by telling us that the maisonette directly above him was vacant and, if we were interested, he would inquire on our behalf. John and I were thrilled. We weren't used to living in such a swinging place as London, so to be able to find accommodation in the same building as a friendly face, who also knew London like the back of his hand, was an added bonus. We looked the flat over and decided it was for us, perfect. Our new London address was to be Emperors Gate just off the Cromwell Road in Kensington.

Moving into our very own place again was wonderful. The thrill of having enough money for the first time in our married life to buy the carpets and furnishings meant that I really had a heyday choosing colour schemes, new china, pots and pans—in fact all that was needed to make the place like home. I found the transition from the quiet life that I had been used to, to a world brimming over with exhilarating speed, excitement and interesting characters very much to my liking. And Brian was just marvellous. He had very quickly acquired gourmet habits and introduced us to the best restaurants in London. The high sophisticated life-style suited his extravagant self-indulgent moods to perfection. He blossomed in new-found confidence. It was as though this was the only way to live and it fitted him like a glove, almost as though he had been born to it. As we moved to London in Brian's wake, so did the rest of the lads. It was the only sensible move to make. Brian took a lease out on a very swish apartment in Knightsbridge. It was in a new block of apartments with one or two flats still vacant. When Paul, George and Ringo saw it, they wanted one too. No sooner said than done, they quickly moved in. Money was really flowing into the coffers by this time with two hit songs already chalked up and one more in the pipeline. They were really big business. Brian excelled himself in the role of manager and entrepreneur. He shone like a star and arranged big business deals with charm and modesty, a very complex character was Brian. He was a most generous man, thoughtful to the point of embarrassment at times, shy and gregarious at the same instant, but if John ever refused him a request he could behave like a spoilt child and throw tantrums, even stamping his feet with frustration, tears in his eyes. And no one could frustrate Brian more than John. I think he revelled in his power to make Brian squirm and lose his temper, even though he admired Brian as manager and godfather to our son.

Life in our new home slowly settled into a more relaxed routine. I did very routine things like housework, shopping, cooking and taking care of Julian and John. I did come across one awful problem though. When we first looked at the flat, we didn't even think about the difficulties of access. Our maisonette was on the top floor of the terraced building. Two other maisonettes were below us which meant as there wasn't a lift we had to walk up six flights of stairs. It was exhausting for me particularly when I returned from shopping with Julian. Climbing up six flights of stairs with a heavy child and bags full of shopping was no joke. The back of the flat overlooked the underground railway and the new Air Terminal so the only way in was the front door. At first this inconvenience wasn't too bad, it was when the fans found out our whereabouts that life became unbearable. We were trapped like caged animals. Girls of every shape, size, colour, creed and nationality would sit on the steps of the building in all weathers clutching autograph books in their hands. Once more I

103

found myself in a state of continuous siege. It was nerve-wracking. Every time John or I ventured out we were pounced on. The screaming hysteria would deafen us, hands would grab, stretch out and touch, pull at our clothes. Poor Julian would disappear from view as they crowded in on his pram to gain a close-up, all one could see was a mass of knickers, bottoms and laddered tights all colours of the rainbow.

'Oh, Cynthia, please can we touch you, please, please will you let us take a photograph of you and Julian. Where is John, Cynthia, do you think he would come out and just wave to us. He doesn't have to speak, we just want to see his beautiful sexy face.'

Passers-by would stop and gape in amazement at the scene they were confronted with. Without being rude to the girls I would try to keep them happy and placate them until the appropriate moment came for me to flee. Shopping was never like this in Hoylake.

On many an occasion the main front door would be unwittingly left open by other tenants, only for them to come home to streams of teenagers complete with sleeping-bags, sandwiches and thermos flasks, settling down for the long night in anticipation of a glimpse of their idol. Opposite our maisonette there just *happened* to be a students' hostel which also proved to be a damn nuisance. On the top floor, which overlooked us, was a balcony. At any time of the day or night you could glance out of the window only to observe groups of youth precariously balancing on the small balustrade, waving, cheering and shouting abuse across the street. It really was an experience I could have done without. I bet the poor neighbours were relieved to see the back of us when eventually we left.

Not only did we have to contend with the constant noise and disturbances from the front of the building. No relief was to be had at the rear either. The underground trains rattled every window in the place and one night when I was alone with Julian the Air Terminal caught fire. I just stood transfixed cradling Julian in my arms, the fierce flames colouring everything bright red. Even Julian's bedroom would suddenly grow light as the flames opposite leaped ever higher into the sky with incredible force. The wind was blowing in our direction and thousands of sparks flew menacingly onto the roof-tops of our building. I was terrified. Bob and his wife, realizing that I was alone, rushed upstairs to reassure me that everything was under control. It took me quite a while and a very stiff drink to settle me down that night. And it took the firemen a long time to contain the fire—even as I went to sleep it was still smouldering.

During our relatively short stay in Emperors Gate so many marvellous things took place, the first being *A Hard Day's Night*, the Beatles' first film. It was filmed basically to showcase their music and talent as songwriters. The script itself depicted an almost true-to-life description of the lives of four very popular members of a group and the problems and hysteria that followed their every move. Dick Lester was the director and the cast contained quite a few famous names, in fact it promised to be a huge success.

John went through hell making that film, he had to be at the studios at a very early hour and John hated getting up early. He would be chauffeur-driven to the studio with the rest of the boys and return home at about seven at night exhausted, only to find the place in a stage of siege. The fanatical girls would by now be getting desperate after having waited all day and would leap onto John with all the ferocity and strength of a bunch of wild animals, claws at the ready. They would kick each other, scratch and bite in order to get closer and if it hadn't been for the size and strength of John's chauffeur Bill Corbett, he wouldn't have got home alive. Before he could get in though he had to open the door with his key, and a favourite delaying tactic by the girls was to stuff the keyhole with chewing gum. John had so many scarves and ties forcibly ripped off him on these occasions that when he eventually fell exhausted into the flat he was bruised and battered and wondering if it was all worthwhile.

'Christ, Cyn, we'll have to get out of this death-trap before they kill me, I had no idea it was going to be like this. It's like a bloody madhouse out there, we deserve every penny we get.'

George, Paul and Ringo were also having fan problems

and in such a high-class area it just wasn't on. The neighbours were paying a great deal for the privilege of living in Knightsbridge and were not going to put up with the scruff of the land camping outside their property. Complaints poured in by the minute and fell on deaf ears. They were having the time of their lives. Although the kids bugged them all the time, they could put up with that as the compensations for them were out of this world. Three young handsome very eligible bachelors were in their element. The demand for their company was beyond belief, beautiful model girls clamoured to be seen in their company; invitations to dinner poured in from leading celebrities. Can you imagine how impressed they were and how their egos grew? It was like a dream come true. Three Liverpool lads ·endowed with everything other than the social graces. They really were a shot in the arm of their hosts and hostesses. Totally unimpressed by bullshit of any kind and ready to shock at the drop of a hat. Their curiosity value and forthright honesty endeared them to one and all. When all were together, their repartee was second to none.

'Hey, John, which knife and fork do you use?'

'I don't bother, I eat with my hands.'

'Hey, Paul, what do you do with this?' (on being handed a hand bowl).

'You bloody drink it, don't you? I have.'

Doing the right thing at the right time didn't have any effect on them, their humour broke down all social barriers.

Brian loved to surround himself with the rich and famous. His parties were always successful, crazy but successful. He loved sparkling stars and was totally addicted to show business. The cut and thrust of business dealing and the glamour of the life was a perfect combination to keep Brian on his toes, and in his element.

During the filming of *A Hard Day's Night,* the only way we could relax and unwind was by going out *en masse* to dinner at some very expensive restaurant. It had to be expensive, a place where the clientele were protected from the ogling and pestering of the general public. All our simple pleasures of the past were definitely ruled out. The cinema or theatre were out of the question unless we could arrange a private showing, which often entailed too many complications for it to be worthwhile. We began to live a cocoon-like existence that was wonderfully entertaining but very restricting. It appeared, for example, from the evidence on the solicitor's desk at this time, that Paul had been a bit of a town bull in Liverpool. Claims for paternity suits rolled in. He found himself in great demand in more ways than one. Whether the claims were true is anybody's guess but luckily for Paul he had Brian and a good solicitor. The scandal soon blew over.

George's love-life, on the other hand, was really taking a turn for the better. He really hadn't had a great deal of experience prior to his move to London but all that was to change. In the film they were making was a very pretty model called Patti Boyd. It was her first role in a film and was the beginning of a very big role in her life. George was in love; he was smitten. Patti, on the other hand, was well and truly involved with a very steady boy-friend. The challenge to George was irresistible. She had everything he wanted in a girl. Looks, style, experience; he *really* fancied her. George proceeded to work to a plan of campaign to woo Patti away from her steady and make her his own. To have a girl, with Patti's looks, figure and experience of life was just what George needed for his image. She would adorn any man's arm.

By the time *A Hard Day's Night* was in full swing John had collected a great number of his weird and wonderful stories and poems together. With the help and encouragement of Bob Freeman, he compiled his first book, *In His Own Write*. John spent hours and hours during his free time completing the illustrations for his stories. The originality and individuality of John's style impressed the publishers enough for them to go ahead. Famous name, unusual talent and a way with words combined to convince that the book would sell like wild-fire. It was an overwhelming success and we were thrilled. A Beatle with an intellect only added fuel to the already blazing fire of success. John was immediately hailed as a very interesting writer with great promise. The first copies were immediately snapped up by avid Beatle fans, indeed it sold so well, and its success was so remarkable, that a Foyle's Luncheon was arranged in John's honour. This accolade given to an author by the literary society was indeed a great honour. On the eve of the event John and I, and a few friends, went out for dinner and eventually landed up at the Adlib, a club very popular with pop stars and celebrities. Totally ignorant of what was to be our fate the following day, we drank, danced and enjoyed ourselves with gay abandon until the very early hours of the morning. After about four hours' sleep and a great deal of grunting and groaning we fell out of bed, heads banging, eyes bloodshot and hands trembling. We had mouths like the bottom of a birdcage and hangovers to beat all hangovers. Both feeling sick, we dressed and washed ready for the chauffeur to pick us up and deposit us on the steps of the Dorchester. We arrived consoling ourselves that it was only a luncheon and would soon be over, nothing really that important. How naïve we were. The moment we set foot inside the entrance of that exclusive hotel we were both overwhelmed. Reporters surrounded us firing questions like ammunition. Flashlights blinded us with their non-stop explosive brilliance. We were totally unprepared for the onslaught. John's publisher guided us as best he could through the holocaust of flashing bulbs and television arc lights, cameramen and technicians. But this time we were in shock, two zombies being led to the slaughter. We wanted desperately to turn on our heels and run like hell but we didn't have the energy or courage to do it. From the foyer to the banqueting hall it seemed like a lifetime. On entering, the size of the flower-bedecked hall took our breath away. Hundreds of immaculately dressed people stood up and applauded. John and I were both without our glasses so we stumbled and fumbled our way clumsily through the mass of tables, chairs and literary buffs to our allotted seats on the main table. We were then separated—John on one side of the main body of speakers and me on the other. We were well and truly on our own. It was a sink or swim situation and I decided it was about time I learned to swim. It was the first time I had ever experienced being the centre of attraction, and the fact that I was blind to all the stares and curiosity helped a great deal. My luncheon companions were a most unlikely combination. The Earl of Arran and

Marty Wild. Marty Wild was almost as nervous as I but the Earl of Arran was a treat. He saved the day for me. He was wonderfully interesting and a joy to speak with. His unbridled curiosity and hilarious anecdotes had me mesmerized. I really began to forget my nervousness and banging head very quickly. I even managed to eat something, in between gulps of white and red wine, marvellous for Dutch courage.

When the eating and drinking finally came to a halt, the television cameras and incredibly hot bright lights were once again pointed in our direction and nerves overtook me once more. 'What next?' I worried. I thought the worst part was over but no, it was just beginning. Panicking slightly I asked the Earl of Arran what on earth all the fuss was about and what we were to expect next on the agenda.

'My dear girl, don't you know? Your husband, as the guest of honour at this luncheon, is expected to give a speech,' he explained.

My heart sank into my boots. 'John give a speech? Oh my God we had no idea.' I peered through the bobbing heads and gesticulating hands in the direction of John only to observe a very sick-looking figure, fidgeting with his tie, smiling with embarrassment. There was no escape. The buzzing excitement and expectation grew, all these prominent people had gathered here for one thing and that was to listen to a Beatle called John Lennon give an entertaining, witty, informative speech about himself and his work. I knew John was out of his depth, alone and unaccustomed to public speaking. My heart went out to him.

As the excitement mounted I cringed with embarrassment, thankful that it wasn't me in his position. The cameramen and technicians were ready; the audience were pregnant with expectation, silence was called for, and poor John was toasted and introduced. The literary Beatle.

The silence was deafening and the lone terrified, crumpled figure of John stood up slowly and nervously, his face white and twitching in the glaring lights.

'Ladies and gentlemen,' he muttered. 'Thank you very much; it's been a pleasure.' And that folks was that! He sat down with great rapidity and relief. He just couldn't sit down quickly enough, much to the disappointment and disgust of all who were gathered there. The looks of amazement on everyone's faces was comical. They were totally nonplussed. Slowly, following a smattering of puzzled applause, the silence was broken by the increasing volume of conversation. We were surrounded by indignant people, realizing that that was all they were getting for their money and annoyed by the lack of expected entertainment. Nevertheless they had their pound of flesh when it came to autographs. John and I spent hours signing first copies of his first book. We were surrounded by clamouring ladies and gents eager to obtain signatures on their first editions of *In His Own Write*. It was an enlightening experience for me and I was showered with very nice compliments which gave me a great deal of confidence—something I was very much in need of. 'Do you know dear you could knock spots off Britt Eckland.' It wasn't really such a disaster. The following day the daily newspapers carried a photograph of me watching John make his non-speech, and the expression on my face summed the whole situation up. The consternation was evident—a very serious profile of a very worried wife.

As I said earlier 1964 was an action-packed, incredible year. The première for *A Hard Day's Night* was to be in the month of July. I was so excited at the prospect. I trudged all over London looking for a suitable dress for the occasion and finally tracked one down. But it needed altering and the trouble was that it wouldn't be ready until the day of the première. In fact my mother picked it up for me only two hours before. I was in a flat spin; we were all in a flat spin. Relations streamed into London for the occasion; complimentary tickets were handed out left right and centre; cars and accommodation had to be arranged. Brian's organizing genius was put to the test and turned up trumps. It was a star spangled, tremendously popular occasion. John, George, Paul, Ringo, Brian and myself were driven to the cinema by Bill Corbett, the chauffeur, in all our regalia. The streets were lined with screaming, cheering fans. London was really lit up with the excitement of the event. When we arrived I had never seen anything like it before in my life—I had to pinch myself in case I was dreaming.

Uniformed police were struggling to hold back hysterical over-excited young girls; the traffic had to be stopped and diverted. Before we actually arrived John was absolutely mystified by the amount of people who were creating the traffic jam.

'Hey, fellers, what's happening? Why are all these people around? What's on, a cup final or something?'

He was honestly amazed when Brian informed him that they were all waiting to get a glimpse of him and the rest of the boys going to the première. They all looked fabulous, the fab four were onto another winner. Brian beamed with satisfaction and pride. I smiled and laughed with unadulterated happiness. Flashbulbs popped incessantly and the screaming and cheering was then music to our ears. It was all so unbelievable.

8

... Tomorrow the World

The Beatles' popularity in England was an established fact by this time but on the other side of the Atlantic they were also catching on very fast indeed. Their records were beginning to sell in their thousands. The demand for an American tour by the Mop Tops was increasing. John was over the moon at the prospect. To be successful in America was a dream come true. All his idols in music came from America and the thought of meeting them or of being involved with America had him hopping around with excitement. Eventually Brian, after a great deal of negotiation, shook hands on a tour to commence August 1964. And I was to be allowed to accompany them, I couldn't believe my luck!

The day of departure to America was finally upon us and we were all beside ourselves with the thrill of the whole adventure. I think I must have been the most envied young lady in the British Isles and America that day. I felt like a billion dollars.

The police and staff at London's Heathrow Airport were in for a day to remember. Hundreds of young Beatle fans converged in the early hours on the airport from every corner of Britain. Trying to keep control of the situation and at least a semblance of order were the British bobbies who found the whole situation mildly amusing, until a takeover bid for the airport gained in momentum and size the like of which they had never experienced before. Amusement turned to amazement as the fans began to arrive in their thousands. The little fans were out in force

112

to give their chosen idols the best send off that any British pop group had ever had. Bearing banners three times their size, transistor radios for constant music (and in the hope of hearing a Beatle classic), sleeping-bags and autograph books. Their adventure was beginning too. It was mass adoration on a very grand scale.

On our arrival at the airport amidst frantic, harassed airport officials, police and the media people, a chaotic collection of confused travellers unwittingly caught up in the sheer madness of the occasion wandered around in a daze looking as if the world was coming to an end. When finally we were given the go-ahead to leave our besieged car we were literally swept off our feet into one of the private airport lounges. The noise coming from outside we took to be the screaming engines of a jet preparing for take-off, but we were soon to be informed by a red faced official that the noise in fact was coming from the fans who were now crawling all over the airport, singing and screaming their hearts out for the Beatles. He said as he gulped down his third brandy, he had never seen anything like it in his life before.

In the VIP lounge we were confronted by all the paraphernalia of a television studio which had been set up in readiness for a quick press conference before take-off. The cameras began rolling and the Beatles in obvious high spirits answered the questions thrown their way with great wit and humour, revelling in their highly personal and individual banter. They really were fast becoming the darlings of the British public and their confidence was shining through increasingly on each subsequent important occasion. They were on the crest of a wave. Their unity and loyalty to each other went without saying. Their clowning irreverent behaviour was so refreshing. For once we had a group of musicians who were honest and direct and their image was created because of that. They just couldn't put a foot wrong. I, on the other hand, stood on the sidelines soaking up the incredible scene before me, in awe of it. I was soon shocked out of my reverie, though, by urgent requests for my body to be moved into the limelight.

'Come on, Cynthia love, let's have one of you. Come and sit over here in the light.'

'Hey, John, is it OK if we take a couple of shots of the missus?'

'How about one of you and Cynthia together, John?'

'Oh come on John, it'll make a nice shot.'

In all the confusion and chaos John nodded his assent to the cameramen. It was totally out of character really. His views about his wife and family being subjected to pestering photographers were very strong. Publicity was beneficial to the group but not to myself and Julian. It would mean that we would also become part of the circus. On this particular occasion though he relented. He was too excited to deny anyone anything least of all a photograph of his wife.

The moment of embarkation arrived and we were rushed, feet barely touching the ground, to the tarmac amidst the loudest reception that any performer could possibly want to hear. The airport terraces were overflowing with humanity. 'We love you, Beatles', banners stretched from one end to the other, waving and billowing in the breeze. The screaming adoration was mind blowing for us all. Total immersion in a vat of Scotch whisky couldn't have been more intoxicating. As I was ushered hurriedly into the aeroplane Brian and the four boys stood at the entrance waving, laughing and shouting to their adoring fans and pressmen. The journey to the States was the most exciting journey I have ever experienced. It was one long celebration. Every single passenger on board had some connection with the Beatles' trip to the promised land. Photographers, reporters, musical arrangers. Malcolm Evans and Neil Aspinall, the unsurpassable Roadies for the Beatles from the early days (more friends and buddies to the boys than employees). The champagne flowed, flash-bulbs flashed and everyone chattered non-stop with excitement and anticipation of an event that had been looked forward to for so long. None of us had any idea of the reception that was in store for us until we finally touched down at Kennedy Airport. And when that time arrived sheer pandemonium broke out. The screaming of the jet once more was drowned by the high-pitched hysterical screaming that was coming from the direction of the airport. It was a case of 'Anything you can do we can do louder' on the part of

114

the American fans. The reception was beyond all our wildest dreams. America had succumbed to the invading aliens. They welcomed us with open arms.

'Bloody hell! Christ! My God! Just look at that. Jesus wept! Just listen to that, fellers!' Remarks made out of shock, not disrespect for the Almighty—just unadulterated shock amidst the scramble to obtain a view from the tiny windows of the aircraft. We climbed over every obstacle to gain a better view of the phenomenon of American madness. The lads were in real awe of a situation that they themselves were responsible for. Brian's composure in the face of ultimate chaos was supreme. His control of the situation gained my respect and admiration. He clicked into action, 'John, Paul, George, Ringo, you stay with me. Mal, Neil you look after Cyn. Everything has been arranged. Limousines have all been laid on to take us to the hotel. We won't be going through Customs.' We were all on cloud nine. When the door of the plane swung open the atmosphere and reaction was indescribable. America truly belonged to us.

The journey to the Hotel Plaza in the plush Cadillacs with their air-conditioning and immaculate chauffeurs was an experience in itself.

News bulletins of the Beatles' arrival in the States came across loud and clear from the car radio, heightening the already incredible excitement. The Plaza we soon realized was a very expensive establishment in the centre of New York. New Yorkers had never before seen the like of the madness that had taken over their city. The area around the hotel was virtually impassible. Hundreds of bobby-soxers appeared, bearing photographs and posters of their chosen idols; waving Beatle wigs in the air; wearing T-shirts with the names of the boys emblazoned over the front and back of them. The Beatles had grown into an enormous commercial commodity and someone was making a fortune out of them. The American police found themselves hard pushed, faced with the problem of keeping the mass of singing, shrieking teenagers in line. Royalty couldn't have received a better welcome than the Beatles on that first American tour.

Once the police had managed to bundle us into the

hotel and into the suite we were all to occupy, we managed to catch our breath enough to survey our surroundings with the delight and joy of children with their first toys. The suite was tastefully furnished with modern, comfortable furniture. The colour scheme was rich creams, browns and turquoise and our rooms led off in all directions from the main lounge. But from the moment we arrived, it was turned into Grand Central Station. It was obvious to me from the start that we were all going to need a great deal of extra stamina to cope with the following fortnight. Everything and everyone in America seemed to have gone crazy, a never ending roller coaster ride with all the thrills and quite a few spills.

On the itinerary during our stay in New York was an appearance of the Beatles on the Ed Sullivan Television Show. It was a very much sought after prize to appear on Mr Sullivan's show. Instant fame was the usual outcome. In the case of the Beatles it would seem that they had already established themselves in the throbbing hearts and heads of the American youth, judging by their welcome, nevertheless it was marvellous publicity and a great showcase for their talent.

Virtually prisoners in our hotel we were guarded and protected day and night by the hotel management's security guards. They were posted at the door of our suite, by the lifts, in fact wherever access could be obtained to the boys and their entourage, toting guns and chewing gum, curious and bemused by the whole set-up yet having to keep all their wits about them to prevent the marauding, crafty young fans from bamboozling their way into the suite.

What a bewildering time we all experienced in that hotel. The phone rang incessantly. John and the boys were interviewed by a very famous American disc jockey, Murray the K, on the telephone. They were tickled pink by the fact that they were on the American radio network 'live'. Murray the K had got himself a scoop and it wasn't long before he arrived at the hotel, announced himself and was accepted as an addition to the ever-increasing group of VIP hangers-on. Murray was a middle-aged whizz kid and the boys were bowled over by his fast-talking American slang and his wild, way-out dress. None of us had ever experienced a really all-American DJ before and he knocked us all out with his speed and organizing ability. He just *loved* telling the boys just where it was all at 'Baby'. Murray the K moved in with all the force of a steamroller. The Beatles were like putty in his hands. He adopted them for the rest of the tour. The total charisma of the man and his cheek went unchallenged. Talk about blockbusters, he was the *original* and his radio station must have given him a medal for initiative.

It wasn't long after Murray's introduction to the group that we were inundated with beautiful, willowy model girls who seemed to appear out of thin air. They would stand silently or recline sexily on the plush sofas emitting sultry meaningful looks to the objects of attention. It was so funny observing the scene, the play acting was truly abysmal and they were obviously totally unaware that any of us had any intelligence at all, or of the fact that the Liverpool commonsense was above and beyond all that rubbish. But still I gave them nine out of ten for trying. The boys didn't know where to put themselves half of the time, knowing that they were being set up for the kill. Their facial expressions and off-the-cuff Liverpool wit, their reactions to this onslaught, were a joy to behold.

Although Murray the K to all intents and purposes was feathering his own nest by taking the boys over, he did show us a great time. We enjoyed ourselves so much when he organized a trip to a well-known New York night-club. We danced and drank our way through the night in the company of such stars as Tuesday Weld and Stella Stevens, to name but two. Ringo delighted everyone there by his clowning extrovert behaviour, and he was a great dancer holding the floor a great deal of the night and revelling in his popularity and happiness. Ringo loved America. He was seeing America in a way that he couldn't possibly have dreamed when such a short time before he had been thinking of emigrating. By the time the jollity had come to an end, jet-lag and exhaustion were setting in fast. We were speedily driven back to base to gain energy for the next turn of events, the rehearsals for the Ed Sullivan Show the following day. Weaving our way unsteadily

117

down the corridor of the hotel to our suite a bright young spark of a photographer jumped out on John and I, hoping for an exclusive. But before he got the chance, John threw his overcoat over our heads. The only view the poor unfortunate man had of us was a very funny back view of four legs and two bodies goose-stepping their way into the distance. From beneath the overcoat muffled giggles and stifled laughter rang out, and my face had been saved once more.

The studios for the rehearsal of the show were not too far from the Plaza but trying to organize the trip needed a mastermind like Brian and the co-operation of the American police. The hotel was in a constant state of siege by hundreds of fans. It was on this particular occasion that I almost met my Waterloo. A passageway had been cleared, just enough for us to pile into the cars. The long arm of the law was doing its job marvellously holding back the milling, screaming crowds so that the boys could scramble past. But the moment they were in the car (it had been arranged that I hang back until they were safely in) the police, under enormous pressure of the crowd, broke their line leaving me in the centre of a mass of fighting, pushing hysterical humanity. I thought this is it, love. Where do I go from here? All I could see through the crowd was the worried face of John yelling in desperation to the law to let me in. The police of course didn't know me from Adam and I was fast giving up all hope for my future when I felt myself being lifted, manhandled and thrown bodily onto the laps of the cursing Beatles. Sympathy was not forthcoming, just a strong lecture on survival and a 'don't be so bloody slow next time, they could have killed you'.

Miami was to be our next venue and the thought of the sun and the sea following our stay in New York with its icy temperatures was very tempting. The publicity which followed the Beatles every step of the way was proving to be very exhausting and we were all ready for a break. Needless to say Murray the K hung right in there with us. The Beatles' base was his base, in fact he even ended up sharing a room with George, much to George's embarrassment and consternation. The last thing George wanted was

'Excuse me, are you John Lennon of the er er?'

for people to be 'talking' about him, if you know what I mean.

Miami was another world, a haven for the wealthy retired American. As if by magic, all our free time was taken up accepting invitations to spend our leisure time with nameless faces and nameless people. It was really weird. On one occasion we found it impossible to leave the hotel by conventional means due to the magnitude of the crowds outside and the fact that we could be followed very easily to our destination. A local policeman who had befriended us and was our personal bodyguard came up with a brainwave. A meat wagon. By this time we were all so sick of the inside of hotel rooms however luxurious they were, that we wanted desperately to see something of the wonderful country we were visiting. We agreed, it had to be a good idea. The plan was to bring the wagon to the kitchen entrance where we would sneak unnoticed past the dirty dishes and food stores into our escape vehicle to freedom. We ran for our lives, leapt headlong into the revving meat wagon with our adopted policeman and on into the pitch darkness of the smelly interior, panting with relief at our success. Before we had time to catch our breath the heavy metal doors closed out the light and the over-enthusiastic driver, imagining himself in the role of getaway hood, put his accelerator through the floorboards. We took off like a rocket and being a shade slow I failed to secure a foot-hold or hand-hold onto the bars which lined the interior of the wagon. The moment we took off, my feet left the ground with arms and legs flailing in all directions, and the darkness of the interior suddenly lit up with stars as I crashed-landed against the metal doors, coming to rest in a crumpled heap on the floor.

'What the hell was that?' shouted a blurred shape from the darkness. 'You mean *who* was that, don't you?' I cried as the lump on my head grew. 'I think it's about time I got danger money, don't you?'

When we eventually reached nirvana, the sun was still shining and the home we were entering was really something. It lay on the edge of the sea and was complete with swimming pool and all the trappings of wealth. George Martin and Judy his lovely lady, were there to greet us. It was wonderful to see familiar faces from home again. Our hosts, we were informed, happened to be away, but looking after us was a regular all-American version of Jeeves appearing for all the world like a refugee from the Mafia. He really reminded me of a Chicago hood from the Al Capone era. All he was short of in my eyes was gun holster and hat pulled down over his eyes. Whilst we were all relaxing in the sun and bathing in the pool, Mr Fixit was barbecuing his way through a mountain of juicy steaks with a less than friendly expression on his face and cigarette dangling from his mouth. It seemed to me that his employers had failed to groom him in the art of putting their guests at ease. Nevertheless we spent a wonderful afternoon swimming, water-skiing and generally letting it all hang out, thanks to our absent hosts.

During our stay in Miami a meeting with the one and only Mohammed Ali was arranged. He was training in Miami in preparation for his next big fight and once more it seemed like the whole of the American mass media were there in attendance. Ali was in great form and the boys were delighted to meet him. Mock sparring sessions were set up with him and the Beatles for the photographers and Ali was, as always, marvellous when confronted by the media. It was a great experience for me watching from my ringside seat the clowning and joking, the sheer speed of mind and body. A fantastic combination in one man, all that talent in one small boxing ring. I was a very privileged young lady and the tour of America was a tour of a lifetime for me.

Back in the hotel again I felt the urge to spend some dollars. I was in a frivolous money-spending mood. In the lobby of the hotel was housed a boutique and I couldn't resist the temptation. I knew full well that the entrance to the hotel was still under siege but I felt quite safe since my face was not well known. So I bade everyone farewell and took off for my spending spree. Whilst browsing through the racks of clothes I found myself listening to snatches of conversation from other guests who it appeared had the same idea as me. Those women fascinated me. The majority were grossly over-weight and far from beautiful in their choice of dress, horrendously dazzling

121

bermuda shorts fastened tightly at the waist, bulging thighs and bottoms everywhere. From the neck up their wrinkled prune-like faces were daubed with thick plasterings of lipstick and make-up. Their hair, though, really knocked me out. Each one of them was adorned with a mass of multi-coloured rollers delicately covered by garish chiffon head-scarves. To complete the ensemble, diamanté encrusted sunglasses rested elegantly on their sunburnt noses. I felt positively naked by comparison. The only thing that was missing from my person was my sketchbook. I couldn't help giggling to myself though when I overheard one particular conversation.

'Did you know that that awful group the Beatles are actually staying in our hotel?'

'Oh my Gaad yes, aren't they just too awful, all that hair!'

'It doesn't look as though they wash it to me. They're such a goddam awful sight I just don't know what our kids see in them.'

'And what about that little one they call Ringo, he is so *ugly!* Did you ever see a nose like it? Well all I can say, honey, is that if those four hairy looking finks can make it then how about us having a go.'

'I agree, honey, they look like four monkeys from a zoo especially that Ringo, *what* a name, *Ringo!*'

At that point they all fell about laughing, including me, after my descriptions of them you can imagine why. Before they had a chance to get into conversation with me I beat a hasty retreat only to find myself confronted with a crowd of young fans and a very adamant security guard. I approached the guard with great timidity realizing that I was without identification of any kind. To make things worse the girls were tearfully pleading with the man to let them pass. It was obvious by his expression that he had just about had enough when I walked up to him. Putting on my best English accent I said, 'Er, excuse me, but I would like to pass please, I am Mrs John Lennon, one of the Beatles' party and I am staying in this hotel.' I was immediately surrounded by about fifty Beatle fans, the palms of my hands started sweating profusely and my face reddened with embarrassment as the girls pushed and shoved to gain a closer look.

'Listen, kid,' shouted the guard. 'If I've heard that one once today, I've heard it a million times, you just can't pull one like that on me. I've heard them all.'

I felt such a lemon, a desperate lemon in fact. As I proceeded to try and knock down his stone wall defence one of the girls, who must have had a photograph of me leapt to my defence.

'Hey, man, are you stupid or something? You gotta believe this lady, of course she's Cynthia Lennon, can't you recognize an English accent when you hear one, you dummy.'

The fans were wonderful and they all rallied round in my defence. Photographs were produced and enough support was given to me for the guard to be convinced of my true identity. I was really impressed with their loyalty which I rewarded by signing my autograph for every one of them before I ascended the stairs to my room. I waved my thanks and promised them all Beatles' autographs for their trouble. You scratch my back and I'll scratch yours was the name of the game.

Following our much needed rest in Miami the boys were due to perform a concert in Washington Boxing Stadium. Although we travelled a great deal we saw very little of the United States. What we did see was the inside of hotel rooms, views from fast moving vehicles, and crowds. The Beatles were fantastic ambassadors for Britain, their honesty and enthusiasm in all their interviews and performances filled me with admiration. Backstage tantrums just didn't exist. They were as one in everything, in tune with each other and their public. They even controlled themselves when their patience was stretched to the limits during a dinner given in their honour by the British Ambassador in Washington. It took a great deal of persuasion from Brian to get them to accept the invitation as the whole set-up was definitely not their cup of tea. However, when they finally succumbed, the true-blue British high society abroad treated them like freaks, as only the upper-class British at their worst could do. Scissors were produced by their hosts.

'Oh which one are you? I'm sure you won't mind will you, darling, if I cut a little of your hair to send home to my daughter in boarding-school.' Not bloody likely, Missus. That was it. They left. Protocol or no protocol they weren't going to stand for that.

The concert performed at the boxing stadium was a stupendous success, although it was almost impossible to hear the boys for the screams of thousands of fans. From Washington we travelled by a train crawling with pressmen, film-men and Uncle Tom Cobley and all. The boys spent the whole journey performing mad antics for publicity and for their own amusement. I wore a black wig, trying in vain to make myself look less conspicuous. We were returning to New York in time for the Beatles to complete their first American tour at the famed Carnegie Hall. It was still like a dream gone mad to all of us. Everything seemed to be happening so fast and even at that time I had the feeling that the train of life we were on would crash before long.

Our arrival back home was as frantic as ever. The scenes that we had left behind greeted us wherever we went. The airport hadn't changed at all. The only thing that *had* changed was our acceptance of the incredible hysteria and adoration of the fans, internationally. It wasn't that we were blasé but we had been living with the situation for two weeks non-stop and it was getting to be a habit. England looked marvellous, slow and familiar compared with the speed and exhibitionism of America. England was home and home was where our son was. United once again with Julian, John and I came to the conclusion that we would have to move into the country. Instead of coping with the usual Beatle fans I found that really weird characters were hovering around the flat, sitting on the stairs directly outside the door. I was really quite frightened for myself and Julian. We had no protection from nutcases when John was away.

I began receiving obscene phone calls regularly and I was just about at my wits' end when we finally went out house-hunting in the countryside of Surrey. We chose Surrey because the Beatles' accountant at the time lived in Weybridge and invited us to go and have tea with him and his family while we were scouting around for our dream house. We liked Weybridge very much, just far enough out of London to have the feel of the country with all the advantages of being within distance for John's work. The house we finally settled for was on the top of a hill, very secluded and in the select area of the St George's Hill Estate. A beautiful rambling wooded estate which provided seclusion and privacy for its tenants. The air of wealth and opulence was apparent to all of us on our first visit. It seemed perfect for our needs at that time. The house itself was a mansion compared to anything I had experienced before. It was mock Tudor in design and the grounds contained every possible tree, shrub and flower one could imagine. Old and slightly run down it had marvellous possibilities.

It was obvious to us that it would need a great deal of cash spending on it but at that time the Beatles' success story had put behind us all the money worries that we had ever had. Money was no object and it was worth anything to find peace and privacy from the frantic mobs that seemed to follow our every move. Once the contract had been signed we packed our belongings and left the city for the refreshing green and space of the country. We were thrilled and very excited at the prospect. Everything seemed to point to a grand scale of living. Nothing seemed impossible any more. The cut and thrust of everyday life was fading into a hazy cotton wool-like existence. We were setting ourselves apart from what to most folks was the norm of life and beginning a form of caricaturist's idea of how a wealthy pop star should live. A rags to riches situation which was difficult for me to comprehend or to fight.

It was as though we were being taken over and the tide of events made us all act before we had time to think straight. Don't get me wrong, the whole experience was truly out of this world, so much so that it seemed unreal.

From the beginning we were advised to employ the services of a reputable interior designer which of course we did without question. The man was overjoyed he had *carte blanche.* John was an impatient man now that the pressures that fame was heaping on his young shoulders

125

gave him little time for cosy chats about what colour curtains he preferred or which type of central heating system would suit. All John could think of was his music and a home finished and ready to live in as quickly as possible. The designer went wild with his new found freedom and no limit to cash supplies.

The first nine months in our new home were spent occupying the staff flat at the top of the house. An army of workmen arrived and proceeded to tear the place apart. The beautiful designs that were presented to us seemed a long way from reality as we wandered through rubble-filled rooms with ripped up floorboards and what seemed like hundreds of workmen's tin mugs and billy cans. In fact we were the mugs. I can't remember inspecting the house when the men were working, they always seemed to be sitting, gossiping and drinking endless cups of tea. I felt like a foreigner in my own home. I kept having to remind myself that we were paying for it all. Apart from the discomfort of living on the top of a building site our dreams of peace and seclusion were soon to be shattered.

Living in the upstairs flat wasn't too bad really but it was almost like living in a high rise flat. At times we couldn't see or hear anything that went on downstairs being cut off from everything. At night, after the workmen had finished their day's work, I would settle Julian and we would spend a very simple evening together watching TV. Everything was fine until silence fell over the empty shell of our home, then our imaginations would run riot at the slightest sound from below. We would argue about who should go and investigate (I told you John was a coward), it usually ended up with us both going—but never farther than the top of the stairs and then we would panic and rush back into our bedroom and pull the bed-clothes over our heads so that we wouldn't be able to hear anything. It was on a morning following such a night that I have just described that we both definitely heard noises coming from downstairs. I rushed down to see what it was only to come across about twenty or thirty young fans climbing their way up to our rooms. The front door was wide open and when they caught sight of me bearing down on them they let out an unholy shriek in unison and fled as

126

though they were being chased by the devil himself. John and I groaned with the agony of it all. Our cover had been blown. We weren't safe even though we were miles from anywhere. It was going to be the same old story wherever we went. We would just have to accept it and go on with it.

Resigned to our fate we got on with the routine of life once more. I had a lovely son who needed constant attention and John had to work as usual. George by this time had been very successful in his wooing of Patti, and everything was coming up roses. The steady was ditched and George was hitched. Trying to keep his blossoming relationship out of the newspapers was virtually impossible and to combat this, in the vain hope of getting to know Patti more intimately, George suggested that the four of us took off for Ireland for a sneaky weekend away from it all. Secrecy had to be the key word.

The arrangements were to be as follows: John and George were to disguise themselves with false moustaches, scarves and hats. A six-seater plane was hired and a suite of rooms were duly booked at the Dromoland Castle Hotel in Ireland. On arrival at Manchester Airport the charade began, trying hard not to lose our self-control in the face of the curious public who, when confronted by a pair of inspector Clouseaus rushing conspicuously through the airport followed by two equally conspicuous giggling females carrying mounds of hand luggage, stood and stared in disbelief. Obviously aware of who they were seeing but not able to put a finger to their identity, we made it to the plane without being apprehended and we clambered into what seemed to me to be a car with wings. I was really terrified, it was so small and vulnerable. I closed my eyes as we took off and had them closed for most of the bumpy journey.

The Dromoland Castle Hotel was a heavenly retreat; it was perfect. Miles from anywhere and very high class. Our suite of rooms had been occupied not long before by President Kennedy or so we were informed. Patti and I got on famously. She was a friendly bubbly character, a great girl full of fun and boundless enthusiasm, very childlike but in no way immature. She always reminded me of a

127

very beautiful flimsy butterfly. I envied her, her figure, her dress sense and her confidence. Whenever fashions changed Patti was in there first with all the right gear looking beautiful as ever. George, I thought, was a lucky fellow. Patti handled George very well considering their different social backgrounds. George's northern bluntness and lack of tact must have been hard to come to terms with in comparison with the smooth southern sophistication of the escorts she would have previously experienced. I liked Patti very much and it was lovely to have female company once more.

Our first day of freedom and peace from the rat race was enjoyed by one and all. Exploring the hotel and grounds without having to look over our shoulders gave us a sense of false security. At last we thought we had cracked it. The evening meal passed without a hitch and we retired to our respective beds safe in the knowledge that tomorrow would prove to be just as beautiful and relaxed.

Dawn broke, the phone started ringing, the curtains were drawn, and before we had time to rub the sleep out of our eyes we realized that we were surrounded. That we were in a castle was very apt, but instead of being confronted by the enemy bearing bows and arrows they were armed with cameras. Holed up in the grounds of the hotel wherever you looked, they pointed their weapons in at us in a very threatening manner.

'Bloody hell, what have we done to deserve this, man.' Note the Americanism, one trip to America and they were anybody's.

'Where the hell do we go from here for Christ's sake?' We were at our wits' end to know what to do for the best, how to avoid being shot and done for by a camera as it were.

Following a deep discussion on tactics we decided the best thing to do would be to appeal to the management for assistance. Only the Irish could have come up with the solution that enabled us to foil our adversaries. It was brilliant in its simplicity. To prevent George and Patti from being photographed together we would have to split up. John and George were to go to the airport alone by conventional means, and Patti and myself were to be

128

smuggled out of the hotel Irish fashion. Everyone entered into the spirit of the operation. Patti and I were to dress up as chambermaids. Black dresses, white frilly caps and aprons, we donned our disguises and stood admiring each other, it was great fun. The idea was for us to carry large bundles of dirty laundry in a large wicker laundry basket down to the staff entrance to the hotel. The staff would keep a look-out for the enemy while the laundry basket was emptied and the two of us climbed in. You can imagine we felt like a couple of jack-in-the-boxes as the lid was lowered and secured tightly above us. The plan in its original form was for the driver of the laundry van and a member of the staff to carry the basket, with us safely inside, to the vehicle. Once inside he was to have released us for the journey to the airport. Everything went according to plan until we felt ourselves being dumped very roughly into the back of the van followed by shouts of panic and confusion all around us. Before we knew where we were, the van doors were slammed quickly and resoundingly shut, the engine was put into gear and we were away. The ride I experienced in the meat wagon didn't hold a candle to that journey.

'Cy what is happening? Where are we going? We'll suffocate and die in this thing. *Shout, Cyn. Shout!*'

In vain we yelled at the top of our panic-stricken voices. '*Help, help,* let us out! Driver you've forgotten to let us out.'

As the van rounded bends and speedily took corners the basket we were trapped in slid from side to side of the clattering van, no way was the driver going to hear us, he was too caught up in the excitement of the escapade. Exhausted and hoarse we gave in with arms, legs, and feet crunched up in the most unlikely positions. We completed the journey feeling like a couple of redundant acrobats from Billy Smart's circus. In spite of our excruciating discomfort our ruse proved to be a great success. I don't know how long it took the poor miserable drenched reporters and photographers to twig that we had flown the coop. At least we weren't in the vicinity to hear the swearing and cursing that must have occurred when they found out we had made fools of them.

As work on our home progressed, John and I began for the first time to experience some semblance of a family life together. Although the intrepid fans still embarked on their pilgrimages to our home, we had more time and more patience to cope with the situation. For me the problem of taking care of an enormous mansion, a pop star husband and a small boy was eased by the daily presence of a lovely lady called Dot. Dot was employed by the previous tenants to do odd jobs and ironing a couple of days a week. Little did she know how her peaceful, ordinary existence would change when she accepted my offer of work in the Lennon household. Dot was marvellous with Julian and in fact with everything. She became expert at virtually everything to do with the madness of being on the fringe of a Beatles' life-style. Living so far away from Town created the need for a suitable chauffeur. Our first big blunder arrived in the shape of Jock. God only knows who his previous employer was because John took him on in his usual impulsive fashion not bothering about such an unimportant thing as a reference. By this time of course we were the proud owners of a Rolls-Royce. Neither of us had passed our driving tests so Jock got the job. I don't think the man had a decent suit to his name. When he arrived to drive us anywhere he looked like an old tramp, crumpled clothing, hair awry, unshaven, very unprofessional looking. John didn't give a damn. He gave Jock full charge of the car and allowed him the use of it when off duty. It was only by chance that we discovered why he was such a mess and why the car stank of ciggies and booze when he rolled up at the house. Apparently a local inhabitant had passed the car night after night parked along one of the estate roads, lights out and Jock curled up on the back seat fast asleep. Our car was his home and his transport for boozy nights out with his mates. What a character! John and I were no match for the con agents. He didn't have the time and I was hopeless when it came to asserting myself.

Our next blunder as far as staff were concerned was employing a married couple. How cosy we thought, a smart chauffeur and his wife as cook and housekeeper. I was quite capable of cooking but when money comes in the door commonsense goes out of the window. We did what we thought was the right and proper thing under the circumstances. Before long Dot and the lady in question were at each other's throats, the chauffeur was flirting with everything in skirts, the married daughter of the couple left her husband and moved in with her parents. Talk about happy families, it was chaotic. You could cut the atmosphere with a knife. Accusations of dishonesty, threats of violence, actions of sneaky revenge. I found myself, the mistress of the house, totally inexperienced in the art of dealing with such crazy people. What really did it for me was the fact that John was God. After all he was signing their very generous pay cheques. I was only the quiet little woman who wouldn't say boo to a goose. When John was home for meals the kitchen would be a hive of creative industry, the food presented would be fit for a god. When John was on tour, Julian and I were presented with frozen chips, hamburgers and peas. Quite a contrast, don't you think? It was my guess their own table was never short of the best fare. So, it wasn't very long before that little group of opportunists found themselves out on their ear.

The interior designer having done his job of transforming our mansion into a very plush and modern home left, with I'm sure, a healthy bank balance. It was very beautiful but my mother still couldn't resist buying us more and more junk and the uncluttered design grew more like home as the months passed. In their bachelor flat in London, Paul, George and Ringo lived it up like there was no tomorrow. Brian found himself in all sorts of weird and wonderful relationships, his parties gained in momentum and madness. From strong drink to soft drugs, from Liverpool buddies to international dropouts, and leeches. Brian was no match for the devious, plausible companions who wangled their way into his generous existence. Luckily for Ringo he had a girl-friend of true scouse stock back home in Liverpool. Although whilst in London he gallivanted around with one of the prominent models of her time, Vicky Hodge, when Maureen arrived in London the smokescreen came down and they behaved like two little love birds. The beautiful occasional birds disappeared from view and Ringo got on with the serious business of courting his true love.

I loved Maureen, she was down to earth, honest and if she had known of Ringo's infidelities while she was in Liverpool I wouldn't have reckoned much to the chances of the girl or girls in question if she had found out. She was madly in love with Ringo and would have fought tooth and nail with anyone who had the nerve to try and take him from her. Ringo knew this, of course, and must have been in a panic many times in case of indiscreet gossip or thwarted lady-friends telling all. As it happened Ringo was lucky enough to get away with it in the face of incredible odds and loyal friends.

In the month of February 1965, Richard Starkey and Maureen Cox, Liverpool hairdresser, were quietly wed. Maureen was in the same condition as I on the day of my wedding although the circumstances were much more settled for them. Their future seemed very secure and it was a very happy occasion for all concerned. The family was growing.

Two down, two to go. The fans, although sad at losing half of a Fab Four to the opposition, were very understanding and loyal. Fan letters arrived by their hundreds. In the main they supported the family group, the rest ignored the fact that wives and children even existed.

'Dear John, I think about you every minute of the day and night. I am lying here in my bed naked, just waiting for you to make love to my beautiful body. I'm hungry for your mouth. My measurements are: 38-22-36, my hair is blonde and it reaches my waist. My friends say I'm beautiful. If you want me any time my address is—'

A Cynthia Lennon fan club was founded and monthly news letters arrived at the house much to my surprise and delight. Paul at this time seemed to be the odd one out on the emotional scene, until he met Jane Asher following one of their London appearances. Paul fell like a ton of bricks for Jane. The first time I was introduced to her was at her home and she was sitting on Paul's knee. My first impression of Jane was how beautiful and finely featured she was. Her mass of titian coloured hair cascaded around her face and shoulders, her pale complexion contrasting strongly with dark clothes and shining hair. Paul was obviously as proud as a peacock with his new lady. For Paul, Jane Asher was a great prize. The fact that she was an established actress of stage and screen, very intelligent and beautiful gave an enormous boost to Paul's ambitious ego. It was as though he was saying to us all, anything you can do I can do better. Jane came from a very intelligent and talented family and Paul was thrilled to be part of it. Jane's mother was a fascinating lady, a classical musician, a real individual who took Paul into her home and made him one of the family. Mothering him and testing him when the occasion arose. Paul was in his element, coming from a close-knit family as he had, his adoptive family filled the gap whilst he was living in London. At last we were all hitched, relationships were taking on a sounder basis.

It was more by good luck than good judgement that Dot turned out to be a marvellous companion and housekeeper, in fact general factotum. Les Anthony, a tall handsome Welsh ex-guardsman applied for job as chauffeur, and John took one look and was very impressed with his size and appearance. He realized that Anthony would be able to protect him in case of attack, so he was accepted. Julian was at the age of pre-prep schooling and began his first term at a local establishment, happy to be mixing with children of his own age for the first time. John had mellowed and life was taking on a rosy glow of contentment, so many new ventures were in the pipeline. A second film, recordings of singles and albums the avid fans craved, and John really had his work cut out for him. Ringo and Maureen decided to move to the country and bought a lovely house on St George's Estate within ten minutes' drive from us. Nights were spent in the recording studios in St John's Wood with George Martin, Mal and Neil, until the early hours of the morning. When the record was in the can, and if it pleased all concerned, a vote would be taken on where to go next in order to relax and rave it up. The proprietors of the 'in' clubs at the time were overjoyed and fell over themselves to welcome the boys and their entourage. Terry Doran, an old Liverpool pal of Brian became a close friend to us all. Terry was willing to do anything, go anywhere. He adored the Beatles and was loved in return by us all. His personality was refreshingly fun loving and when we ventured out and Terry was with us, he was our entertainment.

Due to the pressure of work on John and his natural bent towards the anti-social, I would frequently spend weeks of being virtually housebound by duties to child and staff. John being either too exhausted or bored by the whole idea would suggest that Terry be my escort. Difficulties began to arise due to the difference in life-styles between myself and John. I desperately fought for reality and a family unity in the home. I fought to keep the wolves and jackals from the door of our life. In my mind it was the only way for Julian to feel and accept security, no matter what went on outside the confines of the family. Yet I needed to experience what was happening in the outside world however false and tinsely it was. John would sleep until two in the afternoon most days, eat a hurried brunch and be out to face the speed of decision-making, the creative pursuits of his music, and the meetings with the VIPs of show business. It was no wonder that the thought of socializing put him off especially when he had the chance to refuse. Holidays seemed to be the only times that we really came together and had a chance to satisfy each other's needs without pressure or interruption.

A marvellous winter skiing holiday in St Moritz secured us one such break from pressure. George Martin and Judy suggested it. George was a true gentleman and Judy a perfect lady. George's quiet manner, and shy humour, and tall elegant stature reminded me a great deal of Prince Philip and if you had the pleasure of sitting next to Judy in a restaurant, her voice would ring out more queenly than the Queen. A delightful couple, beautifully matched. Judy was the only one of us to have skied before, so we all started from scratch. Our ski instructor was a very dishy Swiss and obviously fond of the ladies. We had our first hilarious lesson and returned to our hotel for a few drinks in our rooms before changing for dinner. As John and I were about to get changed we heard a lot of giggling and shrieking from the next room, Judy was having a fit.

134

'John, Cyn, you must come here and have a look at George,' another burst of laughter followed. 'Oh, George, you do look an idiot!'

We rushed in to be confronted by George dressed only in his black tights and ski under garments posing with arms outstretched in a very dainty fashion about to attempt a 'pas de deux'. He pointed his long legs in readiness for his dance and promptly tripped. Poor George fell in an agonizing heap at our feet, clasping a badly injured ankle to him like a baby. Whenever I remember that holiday I get a picture of us all rushing into the plush hotel lounge after a day's exhilarating skiing to find George sitting glumly and miserably in an armchair with his foot on a stool encased in plaster of paris.

'Are you all right, George, did you have a good day?' we would ask, trying hard not to show our amusement, 'No, I damn well haven't. If anyone else asks me where the accident happened and on which mountain, I'll scream. I have never felt such a fool in all my life.'

Tahiti was our next memorable holiday, with Patti and George. It had to be somewhere where no one could reach us, no press, no fans, nothing. A yacht was the answer. It was all arranged for us. George was still in the early stages of his romance with Patti and secrecy was still of prime importance. Our mental pictures of the yachting holiday to come were ones of sheer unadulterated, self-indulgent luxury, evenings spent sipping champagne on a sun-drenched lounger on the decks of an Onassis-style vessel. A holiday of a lifetime, in fact a real touch of class. On our way to Tahiti it was necessary to break the journey in Hawaii. The gossiping gremlins it appeared beat us to it. The radio networks were transmitting a blow-by-blow account of our arrival, where we were staying, where we were going, in fact they knew more than we did. The world seemed to be shrinking and we were trapped once more in the confines of the hotel room saved only by an accommodating American lawyer who took pity on us and invited us to be his guests. We spent a very enjoyable couple of hours with our hosts before once more the locals spread the word. The house was surrounded and the police were called to protect us. It was moving on time again. Tahiti would have been wonderful had it not been for the fact that we were greeted with monsoon conditions and a man who wasn't sure which yacht we were supposed to be hiring. He was our contact and he didn't even know what was happening. We were escorted to a quayside bar crawling with cockroaches and asked to wait while he inquired. The time was midnight, the rain was lashing down and we all wanted to go home.

'Bloody hell, doesn't anything ever go according to plan?'

'Who bloody well organized this bleedin' holiday anyway?'

We were beginning to feel cold, tired and totally abandoned when our 'man in Tahiti' arrived with a young man who spoke with an Aussie accent and introduced himself as our cook for the voyage. He had just been signed on for the trip by the owner.

'You will be sleeping in the yacht tonight and we set sail in the morning, you'll meet the rest of the crew then,' he explained.

By this time we were all shattered. It didn't really matter where we slept as long as it wasn't in the street with the cockroaches. As our cook guided us along the quayside our eyes scanned the moorings of our dream boat. We were led disconsolately onto the cramped decks and down into the even more cramped cabin area of an old fishing vessel. Our faces dropped with our spirits but, too exhausted to rebel, we muttered our thanks and fell into our less than luxurious bunks. We dropped off to sleep in spite of the thunderous rain pounding above our heads and the promise of an equally disconcerting day ahead.

When dawn broke the monsoon had turned into a raging hurricane. The cook and Tahitian crew arrived as arranged. The crew spoke no English but could communicate well enough with the cook to inform him that we would set sail within the hour. It was the first time any of us had been on a sailing boat and we didn't know anything about sailing or the sea. But we did all know that it was going to be a very rough crossing to the next island. God only knows how we set sail without capsizing. The crew tackled their work as to the manner born. The land-

'Hey John, Patti doesn't half look like Brigitte doesn't she?'

lubbers, donned in sou'-westers and oil-skins, showing all the signs of turning as green as the broiling sea, hung on like grim death to anything available to save them from falling overboard. The stinking engines were started and we rocked, rolled and reeled away from the safety of the quayside into what I felt at the time was to be our untimely end.

'John, I'm frightened. We're all going to drown. I'll never see Julian again. We're going to be swept overboard. John, I can't stand it, please can't we go back. Tell them we want to go back.'

With the foul smell of burning engine oil and the terrifying enormity of the waves that crashed onto the decks around our feet, I could take it no longer, I sought refuge from the tempest in the cabin while John did his 'Pilot matches' impression of the brave seasoned sailor. He was actually enjoying the experience. I, on the other hand, lost my breakfast and everything else into the nearest available container, which happened to be a brand new flowery sun hat.

I remember very little of that horrendous journey until I came round, looking a very sorry sight. My poor hat was thrown overboard and floated off into the sunset taking all my cares and worries with it. The sea was like a mill pond and the sun had finally decided to reveal itself. When I finally found my sea legs, it turned out to be a truly marvellous holiday. We felt as free as the wind, not a soul to bother us or even to care who we were. The food was far from gourmet. Potatoes, potatoes and potatoes cooked in every conceivable way, the cook's specialty. John and I were the only ones to suffer. We must have gained a stone in weight on that holiday, fat, happy and brown. Patti and George on the other hand were still trying to impress each other in their new found love. George would take John to one side enthusing over Patti and the way she looked.

'Hey, John, don't you think she's fantastic, just look at her, now John, doesn't she look like Brigitte [Bardot]?'

John found the whole situation highly amusing, love's young dream was beyond redemption and if George mentioned Patti's resemblance to Brigitte once he mentioned it a thousand times until he bored the pants off John, being an old married man in comparison to George. Nevertheless we all enjoyed each other's company enormously. Our crew of Islanders were beautiful, simple, happy and always helpful. In fact the holiday instead of turning out to be a disaster proved to be the most relaxing and happy holiday that we ever had.

The trip to Tahiti must have cost us a fortune but by this time money really didn't come into our conversations. It was a fact that Brian and the Beatles were loaded. Everything that was bought and paid for was on account, actual cash never changed hands and John just didn't carry money around with him at all. I don't think he even had a cheque book. It all went down on the bill without a second thought. Christmas time was always a very happy and exciting time. Imagine being lucky enough to be able to buy whatever took your fancy. Two of the most notable London stores stayed open especially for the boys and their families to do their Christmas shopping in peace. It was just like being let loose in Aladdin's cave.

On Christmas Eve, George, Patti, Ringo and Mo would descend on us at our home in Weybridge loaded up with beautifully wrapped parcels. We would drink, talk and listen to records until midnight when we would all go mad and open our respective gifts like silly little kids, oooing and aahing as each gift was impatiently unwrapped, kisses and hugs for everyone amidst shouts of Happy Christmas and Cheers. Julian always stayed up as a treat for this occasion. He would kneel down in the middle of the large lounge, shouting and laughing with delight, surrounded by mounds of wrapping-paper and weird and wonderful gifts of every shape and size. It was always difficult purchasing gifts for our crowd, delighted responses such as: 'Oh fantastic, Cyn, it's just what I've always wanted,' were hard to believe especially when one knew that they all had more than enough of this world's goods already. So the odd, humorous and unusual gifts were always the winners. One particular Christmas, my powers of original thought were wearing very thin until I came across two of the most beautiful carved wooden angels which stood about four feet from the ground. They had been at one time in a church and proved to be very acceptable to George and Paul. For John's fun gift I bought a clockwork bird in a gilded cage which I wrapped up carefully, just leaving the winding mechanism at the base exposed. Before handing it to John I wound it up. The imitation bird warbled loud and clear from its perch as John unwrapped the strange looking gift with an expression of sheer disbelief on his face. Birds were not his favourite pets.

George and Patti decided to set up home together not far from Ringo, Mo, John and I. They bought a lovely home in Esher surrounded by a very high wall. It was happy families time for all concerned, expensive cars were bought and sold at the drop of a hat, swimming pools were built, alterations were made to anything that looked as though it could be improved. It was a time of utter extravagance for the sake of it. It was a peak period of money, talent and emotions, yet it was to change dramatically for me within a very short time.

9

The Beginning of the End

As far as I was concerned the rot began to set in the moment cannabis and LSD seeped its unhealthy way into our lives. Four talented, enthusiastic trend-setters were an obvious target for the underground drug activists. The boys had everything a man could possibly desire in life. Wealth, success, families and true friends who loved them, and yet human nature and the ultimate search for something new and unobtainable in their young lives drove them to experiment with anything and everything that was offered to them. The incredible speed and madness of their success story created a very large vacuum in their day to day existence. As the normality of our previous way of life faded we were forced through circumstances beyond our control into a life-style that none of us could possibly have been prepared for. Although John was happy and satisfied with his music and song-writing the staff flat that we first occupied became full of gadgets, games, bric-à-brac bought at incredible expense on whims of fancy. Anthony, the chauffeur was frequently sent out on errands to buy objects of rubbish at astronomical prices which were frequently used once and left to gather dust. It was a crazy situation which left one with the feeling that this was definitely not fulfilling a true need. It was an exhausting search for the missing element of reality.

Performing all over the country lost its magic for the boys. Totally devoid of their original excitement, they were bored by the monotony of concerts that reduced them to performing puppets in the face of thousands of hysterical fans. They couldn't even hear themselves play, let alone gain artistic satisfaction from music that trapped them creatively and physically into repetitive roles as 'the four Mop-Tops' playing again and again their original hit songs.

In the early days of my relationship with John his humour was grotesque, especially his imitations of cripples and imbeciles. He was obsessed by the horror of deformity, finding it distressing and embarrassing whenever he happened to come across the less fortunate human beings of this life. His drawings intensified his fears and obsession with the ugly. Joking and cartoons were the outlet for his fear. John in no way felt animosity towards the object of his humour but he found that the more popular the Beatles became, the more they seemed to be looked upon as some sort of saviours and shining lights for those who were afflicted with any kind of illness or incapacity. Following each of their performances they would retire exhausted to their dressing-room only to be confronted by queues of wheelchairs containing pitiful victims of polio and other life-draining diseases.

John found himself face-to-face with the victims of his own very real fears, and felt totally inadequate and incapable. It upset him no end; it was too painful a situation for him to be able to cope with; he felt that the whole charade was wrong. He was too irreverent a human being, full of faults and inadequacies, to be raised up in the eyes of these unfortunate people as some sort of saviour. On such occasions his acting ability failed him. It really was too much for four young men to cope with. They were being pressurized into what people wanted them to be, not what they were. Every single thing they did or said was repeated, reported and analysed. Individual freedom had become a luxury of the past. The inevitable step that they took out of their dilemma was a step in the direction of drugs and the resultant freedom of the mind.

Although I was very much a part of the Beatlemania scene I always tried desperately to stand apart, to me it was a matter of survival. I was lucky enough to be able to observe the whirlpool of events without drowning or becoming dizzy. I felt the acceleration of our circumstances grasping us all and preparing to throw us into a confusing chaotic future and I was frightened. John was too involved to be objective and it was always in his nature to take the plunge whatever. The nearer John travelled to the centre of the whirlpool, the farther away I pulled. We became more and more distant in our understanding of each other. I wanted desperately to hang onto sanity; John needed to escape from his reality. He wanted to feel and experience more than the life he was leading offered. I understood completely but couldn't go along with him.

Marihuana was a giggle to the boys and it enabled them to relax. The trouble was that they smoked it whenever they could—on the film sets of their second film *Help*, in the recording studios, at home. It enabled them all to escape from the pressures and responsibilities of their position instead of seeing life in the raw. They enjoyed enormously the view that they had following a puff of a joint. It slowed them down and caused them to laugh at each other and the world. When they smoked the merry-go-round stopped for a while, the world looked brighter, the trouble was that as with anything illicit, such as drugs, along came the inevitable pushers and pimps. Shady characters out to make a fast buck at every opportunity. Brian and the Beatles were perfect bait as were groups like the Rolling Stones, Jimmy Hendrix, in fact all musicians and artistes who had the money to pay for their illicit pleasures. Pot smoking was an accepted and relatively harmless pastime of members of the pop world. But the effect of cannabis on myself was a total waste of time and money. It only made me sick and sleepy. I wasn't lost to the importance of it in the lives of the Beatles though. If they hadn't taken something to relax they would have gone completely crazy.

The possession of drugs and the involvement with drug-pushers was a major worry in my life. At this time the boys took ridiculous risks believing in many ways that they were immune and indestructible, so far from reality had they become, they didn't give their reputations a second thought so caught up in the frantic life-style were they. Pot smoking parties were the norm and the acceptance of the situation and the consequences were all part of the way of life.

Julian's position in this new set up gave me a great deal to worry about. A threat of kidnapping revealed to us by the local police caused many a sleepless night. He was guarded night and day. The police kept watch on his school and our home. Luckily Julian was too young to be aware of the danger he was in, once again the price of fame was rearing its ugly head.

It was when a friend of George's slipped us an LSD 'micky-finn' that I finally realized that I was on my own. It was a horrifying experience that I will never forget, an 'Alice in Wonderland' experience. I felt as though the bottom was beginning to fall out of my world. I never felt closer to insanity than I did then and on subsequent occasions when I took it voluntarily in order to try and understand why John found it so wonderful.

Although my fears, premonitions and insecurities were building up inside me, I kept them very much to myself. I'm afraid at times I gave a very boring, practical impression of an ordinary housewife instead of a swinging, extrovert pop star's wife. I couldn't alter my nature, I just bent it a little in order to try and understand and fit into our new way of life. Don't get me wrong, I thoroughly enjoyed the numerous parties and functions that we attended, tickled pink when I met prominent show business stars and celebrities. Such as the late Alma Cogan for instance who was a marvellous hostess. Her off-stage personality was a very far cry from the impression that she portrayed on stage, a very lovely lady who was extremely fond of the Beatles. It was at one of her parties that I met the late Stanley Baker and his lovely wife, Sybil Burton, ex-wife of Richard Burton, and there was Roman Polanski, Dickie Henderson—you name them, Alma entertained them in great style and with great humour.

John and I also spent many an enjoyable evening in the company of Peter Cook and his first wife dining superbly at their home in Hampstead with such dinner companions as Dudley Moore and that great wit Patrick Campbell. It was all very stimulating and exciting being able to converse and socialize with people who only a few short years before had been names in the newspapers and faces on a screen.

On many other occasions, following a night out at the clubs, John and I would find ourselves carrying on the revelry in homes of people we didn't know, only to find that the lady of the house would set about seducing me and the husband would get to work on John. It was at this point that we would look at each other through our drunken stupor and very quickly take our leave. It appeared that we were very vulnerable to the opportunists and hangers-on of this world who wanted more than anything to jump on the band-wagon of success.

The years 1966-67 were tremendous years of mental and physical change for the Beatles. 1965 had been packed with success following success. Sell-out tours across the world. The highly successful film *Help* was premièred in London in the presence of Princess Margaret and was followed by a fantastic party where Maureen in her final days of pregnancy danced and gyrated the night through watched with great concern by all. It would have been an incredible occasion if she had given birth in the presence of H.R.H. Maureen was enjoying herself more than anyone else; it was her first baby and she was making the most of life while she could.

In June 1965 the Beatles were awarded the MBE. It was a very proud moment for me, my only disappointment was the fact that family was not to be included in the invitation to the Palace. None of the boys wanted their families along. They said that it was going to be complicated enough without having to be concerned about the welfare of an entourage. So off they went to meet the Queen, what more could they possibly do? They had done everything else. The Beatles' success story was without precedent in this country, and they were all still very young men.

A second American tour was then arranged for the boys by Brian, a follow-up to their first fantastically successful visit. Everything was going well until in an interview John likened the Beatles to Jesus Christ. His truly honest assessment of their popularity offended the God-fearing, clean living Americans who lived in the Bible belt of America. His views were totally misconstrued. John was very bewildered and frightened by the reaction that his words created in the States. Beatle albums were burnt in a mass orgy of self-righteous indignation. Letters arrived at the house full of threats, hate and venom. John would come downstairs in the morning and look intently over my shoulder as I opened the mail and ask worriedly, 'How's it going, Cyn? How many for and how many against?' To add to the misery of the impending tour a prominent American and highly successful clairvoyant predicted that the plane carrying the Beatles to America would crash with no survivors. This unwelcome piece of information really gave us all the heeby-jeebies. Our farewells before John embarked on that journey were long and lingering. We were convinced that we wouldn't see each other again. John was sure that if the plane didn't crash, some incensed religious fanatic would pull a gun on him and kill him. It was a very worrying time for all concerned.

In January 1966, George and Patti got spliced. It was so secret that none of us attended the wedding. Paul and Jane were not yet ready for marriage—they had quite a few personal problems to iron out. Jane confided in me enough to say that Paul wanted her to become the little woman at home with the kiddies, but Jane was not prepared to give up her flourishing career as an actress. It seemed that they had both reached a stalemate, so they carried on happily in their own way.

The Beatles, their wives and girl-friends were a very compatible group. There wasn't a single occasion when any of us fell out with each other, the fellers spent a great deal of time with each other at work and play, and were always in harmony. The group was a marriage of four minds, three guitars and a drum, and the girls in the main tagged along and moved in whichever direction they were pointed by their men. The Beatles were very happy to have their women subservient in the background. It made life easier for them. The northern male chauvinism was quite strong within the group and independence was a bit of a dirty word unless of course you happened to be in show business, or someone else's incredibly talented and interesting wife, who just happened to lead an independent existence as well as cope with a marriage. I must admit that we were all to some extent conditioned in our roles, to be seen and not heard. Very Victorian and totally different to the lives they themselves led and the temptations they succumbed to whilst on tour. It was a question of 'don't do as I do but do as I say', and we did.

Maureen was really incredible with Ringo, especially when the boys were recording until the early hours of the morning. Instead of going to bed she would wait up until he came home and serve him a wonderful roast dinner, even if it happened to be five in the morning. I, on the other hand, would spend all morning trying to keep the house quiet in order that John could sleep until the usual two o'clock in the afternoon. I would then creep upstairs and serve him breakfast in bed with tea and the newspapers. They really were cossetted at home.

Although you might think that I had all that any woman could wish for, life could be very lonely. John spent weeks and months away from home; there seemed to be very little time for us to be as close as we were in the early days, and we seemed to be pulling in opposite directions. We never rowed; we just rubbed along together without fireworks. Our bond was Julian but even the simple pleasures of fatherhood were denied him due to pressure of work and lack of time.

It was always a wonderful break in routine for me when prominent pop stars paid us a visit. John did not enjoy entertaining but I loved to welcome people to our home. Admittedly I usually ended up a nervous wreck but I loved every minute when I was on my own territory. Bob Dylan came unexpectedly one night; Joan Baez another. A short stay by Mike Nesmith, of the Monkees, with his wife was fascinating! Until it came to breakfast and she hovered over me while I was cooking, inferring all the time that I wasn't doing it right. 'Mike doesn't like it like that. I always cook it for Mike this way.' How I kept my cool I'll never know.

As with the Beatles Brian too had all that any man could desire, except a permanent relationship with another human being—someone he could trust. He would flutter around like a moth forever getting his wings singed by the tempting bright lights. Brian had achieved the ultimate in accolades, his managerial success was second to none and yet he was full of complexes and insecurities.

It was during 1966–77 that flower power and love children made headlines all over the world. A bloodless revolution created by the youth of America and England. Despite all the beautiful ideals and freedom of expressive and demonstrative love it propagated, flower power was synonymous with drugs, mind-bending, destructive and very dangerous in many cases. Dropouts, communes and hippies were at the mercy of the pimps and pushers. To create a perfect society where peace and love predominated everything they had to turn their backs on the world at large. Commerce and business were dirty words; flowers and music were their means of communication. The Beatles were absolutely in tune with the youth of the world. They led the way and their influence was tremendous.

The press went berserk when, in an interview, Paul conveyed to the world that he had taken LSD. Paul answered truthfully, the press went to town. In my view the newspapers should have underplayed the drug problems. I think instead of dissuading the children from experimenting they fairly fanned the fires of controversy, making the whole scene sound wonderful, illicit and above all exciting. To print the fact that one of their heroes had actually taken a drug was asking for trouble, but of course sensationalism was far more important than responsibility of action. And the results were inevitable. Of course I appreciated the arguments for and against at the time.

During 1966 John was given the opportunity by Dick Lester of proving his worth as a straight actor in the film *How I Won The War*. It was a very strange film in many ways. A galaxy of well-known British actors made up the cast including Michael Crawford. The film was made on location in Spain. Although John accepted the challenge, he could hardly refuse Dick's offer without putting a strain on a very good relationship. John was nervous at the thought of going it alone. The Spanish seaside town of Almaria was the base for the film company. John, accompanied by Neil Aspinall, rented a villa on the coast with Michael Crawford and his wife Gabrielle, baby

148

daughter and Nanny. John promised that I could join him as soon as he had found his feet and settled into filming.

It was a marvellous opportunity for me to mingle with actors and cameramen. To be able to observe at first hand the problems and intricacies, the joy and despair of film making. John didn't take to acting like a duck to water but he really enjoyed the total immersion in a very new way of thinking and performing. Any accolades gained for his performance would be for him alone. He had no George, Paul and Ringo to fall back on for support.

The so-called villa was owned by a baron somebody or other who charged exorbitant rent. The property was damp, tatty and very depressing. It was only when Maureen and Ringo came out to join us for a holiday that we decided to find ourselves somewhere more comfortable, large enough to house us all for the remainder of the filming. After scouring Almaria for days we settled on an enormous villa. It had everything. A swimming pool, which through lack of use was covered with thick green slime, solitude, peace *and,* by the time we left we were all convinced that it was haunted. Apparently the building had originally been a convent. We all felt a very strange presence as we entered, yet no one could put their finger on what it was. But then objects began mysteriously to move in the nanny's room. The electricity kept going off and to top it all Maureen woke up one morning with her nightdress tied back to front in a knot. She had tied the ribbons in bows. She was adamant that Ringo was not the culprit. We decided to liven the place up by having a party for the film crew and actors, hoping that we would shock the spooks enough for them to leave us alone. On the night of the party everything was set for a wonderful night of revelry, following a great deal of shopping and organizing. We all gathered together in a local restaurant and left for the villa, everyone in high spirits. When we arrived, we started dispensing booze for our guests, music was organized for those with energy enough to dance, and everything seemed to be progressing beautifully when . . . the electricity went off and we were pitched into darkness. The weather changed, the wind howled, the rain fell and the lightning flashed. It was like something out of a horror movie. Being used to blackouts we were prepared for the worst and had bought supplies of candles for such an emergency. Although we were all a little disconcerted by events we were lucky enough to be fortified by our own brand of spirits. The hall in which we were holding the party was baronial in its size and atmosphere. When the candles were lit and placed in and on every possible surface, the atmosphere altered dramatically and magically. And it was at this point that I was convinced beyond all doubt that the villa housed many beautiful spirits. The light from the numerous candles danced and flickered with life. The glowing warmth lit up the faces of the guests in an almost religious light and, as if the whole episode had been rehearsed, we all dotted ourselves around the hall in orderly groups and, without hesitation, someone began singing. It was a matter of seconds before the air was stilled and the most beautiful singing you ever heard filled the hall. It was as though everyone there was in total harmony musically and in spirit. It was an incredibly magical experience which lasted for about half an hour by which time, as if an unseen force had snapped its fingers, the lights went on again breaking the spell for one and all. I firmly believe our voices and bodies during that time were instruments and outlets for the nuns' spirits.

Although that particular experience was unheralded we were all fascinated with the concept of life after death and in fact anything paranormal. So it was with great curiosity and interest that we accepted an invitation to a very well-known health farm in the south. It was run by a very interesting couple who were convinced that they were receiving messages from UFOs in outer space. They said that they frequently communicated with them and a space craft had even been sighted landing in the grounds. Their request for us to visit them and listen to the messages with them on their special receiver filled us with fascinated anticipation. On arrival, we were ushered into the dining-room. We wined and dined in the presence of our hosts and another of their guests who was a clairvoyant. The clairvoyant's face was very grey and drained of colour. He was small of build and to me looked not long for this world. I asked him if he was all right to which he replied,

'Communicating with the other world is a very exhausting business. It uses up all of my energy.' He then went on to say that the vibrations I was emitting convinced him that I also had the power to be clairvoyant. It would take time and dedication but he felt that I had the gift. It was quite an unnerving conversation and I thought to myself that although it was all very fascinating, no way did I want to end up looking like him. So I decided there and then that the occult could look after itself without any help from me!

Following a delicious dinner a crackling log fire in the library welcomed us and we relaxed into the plush leather furniture. Our hosts tuned their receiver and twiddled and twiddled and twiddled with the knobs of the set.

'There, can you hear that? We've almost got through. Can you hear them, John, George. They are trying to reach us!'

As we sat listening for signs of anything intelligible or for sounds that any of us could possibly identify, we began to feel very silly and very embarrassed for them and for ourselves.

'I'm awfully sorry, folks, but I think our friends from space are finding it impossible to reach us tonight.'

By this time we were giving each other bemused looks and moving around uncomfortably in our seats, clearing our throats and preparing to leave. Then the clairvoyant suggested that we take part in a séance, seeing as how our visit had so far proved fruitless. We could not refuse without offending our very gracious hosts, so we settled down once more to our fate. As it happened none of us had ever been to a séance before and we were all rather nervous and giggly about the whole thing. The clairvoyant medium sat back into a large leather wing-backed chair. The lights were extinguished and we were asked to hold hands.

Silence reigned, but John made it very difficult for me to concentrate by tickling my hand. All around me I could sense one enormous suppressed, hysterical giggle waiting to explode and I just prayed for self-control. The seriousness of the occasion was totally lost on our little group, until the medium started to make very strange grunting noises. His breathing became heavy and laboured and we all became terrified. We gripped each other's hands with great force, making sure that we were all still there. When he spoke we literally jumped out of our skins. The tiny ineffectual man was standing, his voice the voice of a giant. Our grip on each other tightened and our eyes popped out of their sockets with amazement. The bellowing voice identified itself as a Red Indian spirit. He spoke loud and clear about many things and future happenings but didn't mention anyone by name until he asked,

'Is there a Cynthia one here?'

My heart pounded fit to burst, I found it almost impossible to swallow.

'If there is a Cynthia one here, you must listen to her. The Cynthia one will lead the way.'

Well that was a turn-up for the book, I would lead the way according to heap big Indian in the sky. I must admit I was thrilled to be singled out during the séance, and I think everyone else was slightly peeved not to get a mention. On our way home shouts abounded of 'Rubbish!' and 'It was all a big con, just like the UFOs.' They were all obviously disappointed by the fact that as celebrities they hadn't been made a fuss of by the spirits. I just sat and listened with a smug grin on my face.

'And who wants to listen to you anyway; he must be mad!' was John's response.

John's appearance altered drastically following *How I Won The War*. In the film he had to have his long, beautiful locks shorn. Round, wire-framed National Health glasses rested unflatteringly on his nose. He looked the complete opposite of an adored pop idol. In fact, in the past, John had experimented with contact lenses but they had proved to be an occupational hazard thanks to the foreign bodies and particularly jelly babies that were hurled through the air during their concerts. Time and time again he would lose them on stage or be hit in the eye which resulted in excruciating pain as the lens scratched his eyeball. Now John loved his National Health glasses, ugly as they were. They were individual, like him, and set off a craze for John Lennon specs.

Although filming in Spain had given John and I more time together, our return to England and our time together was to be short-lived. A tour of Japan was on the cards. Julian by this time was old enough to be taken abroad on holiday so while John was on tour it was a good opportunity for me to take my mother and Julian away for a break. Italy was to be our destination, a hotel in Pesaro on the Adriatic coast. My mother had been there before and recommended the place to me. 'It's wonderful for children, Cyn, Julian will love it and no one will know you so you will have plenty of rest and sunshine.' It was in Italy that poor little Julian had his first real taste of Beatlemania, all due to the fact that some clever photographer who must have been tipped off about our holiday took lots of candid happy family shots of me carrying a very frightened little boy from one plane to the connecting flight at the airport. It wasn't long before Italian magazines splashed those photographs all over Italy. If anyone could have done with a strong, strapping road manager it was us. Luckily the owners of the small hotel we were staying at were incredibly kind. There was nothing they wouldn't do for our protection and their names were Signora and Signore Bassanini. Julian was treated like their own child and we were cared for as one of their own family. They took us out to eat at the most typical Italian restaurants; wined and dined us in a wonderful fashion.

Our problems only arose on the beach. One moment Julian would be playing happily in the sand, the next he would be the centre of a screaming crowd of people trying to kiss the Beatle bambino or lift him up. The child was terrified. His screams would alert me to the danger and we would have to make a very hurried and angry exit from the scene. This happened daily. The poor kid became a nervous wreck before the holiday was over, and it was with relief that we returned home, suntanned but far from relaxed.

It was on the tour of Japan that John wrote me a very long letter. He was homesick and missed us both terribly. 'Please, Cyn, do your best for us to be alone for a while when I get home. Try and make sure that your Mum and Dot aren't there.' When John finally arrived home our reunion was closer than it had been for a long time. I think John missed us more due to the fact that Julian and

I had also been away. It must have made John think twice about our relationship. I was also thinking a great deal about the situation we were in. I wanted desperately for John to be proud of me.

As I browsed through the press photographs of myself, I wasn't happy with what I saw. The beautiful, swinging ladies, who were in constant attendance on the Beatles made me look twice at myself and my own image. I tried to work out what single feature caused my lack of self-confidence. It all boiled down to one thing. My nose. I had inherited my father's Roman nose whereas my brother's nose was tiny and feminine like my mother's. I soon became obsessed with my profile, with every photograph of myself I dreamed of blocking out the bump. Until I came to the decision that I have never regretted . . .

'John, I'm going to get my nose done. I hate this one, what do you think?'

John's reply was in the affirmative, 'If it will make you happy, Cyn, go ahead, only don't come crying to me if they make a mess of it.'

So before I had time to think twice about it I went and did it. A new beautiful nose that was all I could think of, a new me. I was convinced my whole personality was going to change dramatically for the better.

Whilst I was lying in my bed in the London Clinic I received a beautiful bouquet of red roses. The card read: To Cyn, a nose by any other name. Love from John and Julian.

The day my new nose was unveiled I was terrified. I was convinced the outcome of my vanity would end in disaster. I would be the laughing stock of everyone I knew. But when the plaster and bandages were removed I was truly overjoyed. John too was fascinated by the new me. The swelling around my eyes and nose gave me the look of an oriental and John thought I looked beautiful. Julian didn't even notice and neither did anyone else. I had to prompt our friends by saying, 'Don't you notice any difference in me?'

'Oh yes, are those new glasses you are wearing?' or, 'Have you had your hair cut?' were the stock replies. The
154

plastic surgeon had done a very good job, he had given me the right nose for my face.

The summer of 1967 saw the emergence of the philosophical Beatles. The regular use of drugs opened up their minds and bodies to an awareness of life so different to the original *She Loves You* and 'boy meets girl' image. Everything and everyone was beautiful as long as they were on the same wavelength, as long as they had experienced the same mind expanding drugs. John strongly believed that everyone should experience the joy of knowing this life, of coming to terms with one's own ego, accepting one's body and mind as being an integral part of the universe. It was like living with someone who had just discovered religion. It was religion but reached as far as I was concerned, by artificial, mind-bending means—a crash course. It was like a Walt Disney nature film where the process of blossoming and growing was shown at high camera speeds. The Beatles' artistic and creative talents blossomed at just such a speed. The psychedelic and hallucinatory qualities of the drug LSD were absorbed and directed into their music; they painted incredibly colourful pictures with words and music. As an artist and musician John found LSD creative and stimulating, his senses were filled with revelations and hallucinations he experienced each time he took it. John was like a little boy again. His enthusiasm for life and love reached a new peak; he had opened the floodgates of his mind and had escaped from the imprisonment which fame had entailed. In many ways it was a wonderful thing to watch. Tensions, bigotry, and bad temper were replaced by understanding and love. The peacock spread its fine feathers, dazzling colours and clothes took the place of conservative suits and ties. It was as though the whole youth movement was shedding its skin and throwing away years of inhibitions, rule and regulations. The Beatles and the Rolling Stones led the revolution without even trying.

As a result of changing mental attitudes our home life also changed drastically. During the making of *Sergeant Pepper* John decided to have the Rolls-Royce painted. Colour and design were of the utmost priority and he employed a firm of barge and caravan designers to do it for

155

him. The idea came to him when he bought an old gypsy caravan for the garden.

There is an expression jazz musicians use when playing with a musician who is not quite in tune with the rest, 'He must be listening to a different drum.' This particular expression adequately describes the way I was feeling at this time. John was still searching, whereas I thought I had found what I wanted out of life. I was frightened and worried by the speed of events and it was becoming almost impossible to communicate with John. The friends and hangers-on who visited our home were also seeing the same visions as John, and if they didn't they put on very good acts in order to get a foot in the door. The private image that John had portrayed for so long gave way to open house parties. He would return home following a recording session and night-clubbing with a retinue of flotsam and jetsam he had picked up on the way. They would all be as high as kites. John didn't know them and neither did I. They all came along for the trip. They would spend the night raving and drinking and listening to loud music, ransacking the larder, dossing down all over the house. The following day the house would be littered with glassy-eyed bodies all waiting to be fed. It was at this point in our marriage that I realized that unless I joined the club we weren't going to survive, so I succumbed to one of John's never-ending requests to take LSD with him and a few close friends. I didn't want to, but I felt that I had to to save our marriage. I also believed that John in his own way was doing the same. Like a seasoned drinker confronted by a teetotaller and wanting desperately to communicate the joys of drink in order to gain a deeper understanding and an even relationship. During my trip John was marvellous. But whatever happiness and awareness John had gained through his own experiences, I did not. I hated every moment. It was hell on earth. Losing control of my mind was the most horrifying feeling I have ever experienced. The hallucinations sent me into renewed panic. Through my tears and fear I would look at John in the hope that he could in some way help me out of the prison that my mind had become, only to see the man I loved changing into a slimy snake or a giant mule with

156

razor sharp teeth, leering and laughing at me. All the time John would tell me how much he loved me and that he would never leave me. All I could reason was that I was definitely going mad and that I would never regain my sanity. It was traumatic and horrendous and only when the drug was beginning to wear off did I begin to feel safe again, secure in the knowledge that the torture would soon be over.

It occurred to me when weeks had passed that I had fought every moment of the time I was under the influence of LSD whereas those who professed to gain something from the experience just let it happen. They totally succumbed to the effects and enjoyed the beauty of their hallucinations and feelings. My innate instincts for survival did not allow me to accept the unnatural. I couldn't accept that drugs were not dangerous. I had seen too much insanity and changing personalities to believe that they didn't do any harm. As far as I was concerned drugs stripped away one's protection and individuality, qualities that stop us from all becoming sheep. They set the users apart as a super-aware élite and instead of enhancing human relationships, they ultimately destroy them.

My premonitions of our life crashing were fast becoming reality. For all the pain that I had experienced and for all John's dedication to getting us on the same wavelength the results put us back to square one. The brick wall was growing higher between us.

Having bought a dream country home, complete with butlers and housekeepers, Brian decided to hold a party. Many well known celebrities were invited. We *all* loved Brian's do's. It was arranged on the day, a Bank Holiday that we all travel down together in the psychedelic Rolls-Royce. We were packed like sardines inside the hot and very cramped car, and everyone was in incredibly high spirits. It had all the feeling of a school outing. Every time the car passed through town or villages it stopped the traffic. Crowds of jeering, waving people pressed up against the tinted windows trying to get a better look at the occupants of this crazy car. It was like travelling in a time machine. The boys were smoking pot and even if you don't smoke it yourself, breathing in the fumes can affect you in

157

much the same way. A pill was passed around and everyone giggled stupidly and had a nibble. It was very hard for me to explain what the atmosphere was like in that car at the time. I can only describe it as insane, freaky, self-destructive, irresponsible. A contagious mood that spread like wildfire in the dark, squashed confines of that crazy vehicle. It seemed unreal—the faces and hands pressing against the windows at each stop only accelerated the madness that we all felt.

After my self-confessed fear of drugs I find it almost impossible to justify my irrational behaviour during that journey. In biting the communal pill, knowing it to have been LSD, I can only say that the feelings of togetherness and unity of atmosphere in the car gave me a very false feeling that *now* was the right time to hear John's drum. It was now or never. Perhaps a miracle would occur and everything would fall into place again as far as our relationship was concerned. I had already realized that any positive move, as regarded our future together, would have to be made by me. Once again I had gone against my better judgement. I found myself in strange surroundings with strange faces staring at me. I tried to fight once again the influence of something stronger and more powerful than my self-control. I sat tongue-tied, paralysed with self-imposed shackles. When John moved away from me I followed hoping that he could in some way comfort and support me. But John was not happy; he was not enjoying the experience as he had before. He ignored me and glared as though I were an intruding stranger. I felt desolate. I sat on the windowsill of an upstairs room contemplating the long drop to the paving-stones below, musing to myself that it wasn't really that far down and that I could even jump. I was drifting off into a very deep depression when someone called my name and I was snapped out of my apathetic reverie. Even though I was under the influence of the drug I knew that all hope for John and I carrying on with our marriage in the same vein flew out of that upstairs window with my thoughts.

Brian's party was like the mad-hatter's tea party; everyone was crackers as far as I could see. They were all mad including me.

A young Greek entered our lives during this crazy period, he was introduced to John by John Dunbar, Mariane Faithful's estranged husband. John Dunbar praised this young man's attributes to the skies. Alexis Mardas was an electronic engineer—Magic Alex. Magic because of his so-called wonderful, wayout inventions. He was a truly plausible person, and had the face of an innocent. His hair was as blond and as angelic as his smile. John was knocked out by Magic Alex. To John, who was totally ignorant of the tricks one can make with electricity, he believed that Alex really had something magic about him. He believed every word that he said.

> *A flower, a kiss, a smile of love*
> *Heartwarming gifts from up above.*
> *The hand of coldness disappears*
> *When we forget our chosen fears.*
>
> *Just one experience of love*
> *Gives hope and life in endless years*
> *Of learning how to move our minds of stone*
> *When many times we feel alone.*
>
> *We are alone. The choice is ours,*
> *To offer a flower, a kiss, a smile*
> *Is but the simple answer, for while*
> *We search our minds in depth*
> *We should find life a simple test.*
>
> *When realization of the truth,*
> *Presents itself in all its youth*
> *To all in age who still ask why,*
> *Just smile and love but do not cry.*

10

A Cosmic Awakening

Alexis gained himself a very strong foothold in the Beatles' camp and although I didn't dislike him I did take everything he said with a pinch of salt. I am too cynical by nature to believe everything people want me to believe and Alex was really out to impress. It was his need to impress that led him to introduce us all to another kind of magic, Meditation. The Maharishi Mhahesh Yogi was in London giving lectures on his own particular brand of Transcendental Meditation. Alexis had heard of him before and suggested that the Beatles go along to the lecture to observe at first-hand the wise teacher from India. The fact that he had any influence at all over the Beatles was a feather in his cap.

I must admit that the best thing that he ever did in my eyes was to point the boys in the direction of the Maharishi and away from drugs. Although I don't believe he had any idea that the Maharishi would become such a strong influence on the boys, leaving his particular brand of magic out in the cold as it were.

It was a lucky turn of fate that the Maharishi was who he was, where he was and when he was in our lives. The pace at which we were living, a surrealistic existence in anyone's book, would have proved disastrous if we hadn't found someone like the Maharishi to put the brake on for us. Brian's life-style was also accelerating at a breakneck speed. He was almost becoming redundant as far as his managerial prowess was concerned. The Beatles were worn out, fed up with touring, and were only planning to record in the future. Their whirlwind success had all got out of hand and they needed desperately to do their own thing more often. Public appearances stopped and Brian was in many ways left on the shelf. It seemed that he had done his bit and he would have to come up with something else which would excite the boys and involve them in business with him. The idea Brian came up with was a company called Apple. His idea was to plough their money into a chain of shops not unlike Woolworths in concept—Apple boutiques, Apple posters, Apple records. Brian needed an outlet for his boundless energy. He wanted to be wanted. I'm sure he felt in some ways that he was losing the Beatles. Although Brian listened to the boys' excited, enthusiastic rantings about the Maharishi, for the first time Brian did not show any personal interest in his group's activities. He nodded, smiled and listened, but did not want to be involved himself. When I look back, Brian must have felt many pangs of sadness at seeing his boys take off without him for the first time in six years. He *must* have seen, as I did, the beginning of the end.

I believe the Maharishi put peace and harmony back into our lives. Although I wasn't present at the lecture that he gave I heard all about him from John, he was open and ready for a good influence in his life and Maharishi seemed to fit the bill. The thought of reaching mental highs without the help of drugs really grabbed John's imagination, and mine. It all sounded so wonderful and *harmless*. The Maharishi's next lecture was to be held in the college in Bangor, North Wales. John and George were really hooked on the idea, Paul and Ringo merely interested. In delighted enthusiasm they asked the Maharishi if they could stay in Bangor with him to do a weekend course. The Maharishi was overjoyed. To have the world-famous Beatles as converts must have filled him with delight. What better publicity could he ask for than that? It was on August 26th that the train, bearing Beatles, Yogi, friends and families, not forgetting the ever-vigilant reporters and photographers, left London's Euston station from platform 8—leaving guess who on the platform. It was all so stupid. It was in our car that we drove at breakneck speed to the station. It was I who was ready hours before anyone else, yet I was the one who was barred from scrambling onto the train as it began to move out of the station. As the biggest policeman you have ever seen pushed me aside, I shouted desperately for someone to help. It just wasn't fair. I watched tearfully as the train slowly drew away from the platform. If I hadn't felt so miserable I would have laughed. John realizing that something was missing from his baggage poked his head out of the window and other heads sprouted their way out to see what was happening. John's face was a picture. He just couldn't believe what was happening: 'Tell him to let you on; tell him you're with us!' His voice became fainter and his face a disappearing blur as the train rattled into the distance. Being an emotional female I burst into tears. I found it really very embarrassing. Brian's secretary put his arm around me in an effort to comfort me in my hour of need telling me not to worry, that Neil would drive me to Bangor and that we would probably get there before the train arrived.

What nobody could possibly understand was that my tears were not because I had missed the stupid train but they were expressing my heartfelt sadness. I knew that when I missed that train it was synonymous with all my premonitions for the future. I just knew in my heart, as I watched all the people that I loved fading into the hazy distance, that that was to be *my* future. The loneliness I felt on that station platform would become a permanent loneliness before very long, I shivered at the thought. Although the journey to North Wales was very enjoyable I couldn't shake off my feelings of impending doom. It was awful. I chatted and joked with Neil in order to take my mind off my fears. Our arrival was greeted with hugs and kisses and derogatory remarks like:

'If you want to know the time ask a policeman, but don't miss the train while you're doing it.'

'Why is it that you always seem to be last? What's the matter with you? For goodness sake get in the front next time.'

That night was spent unpacking and anticipating, with a great deal of excitement, our initiation into meditation with the Master himself. Mick Jagger and Mariane Faith-

162

ful were also in on the new mental turn-on. We were all very happy and impatient to get on with it. The lodgings provided at Bangor were less than luxurious, but very adequate for us all. It was marvellous feeling like a student once again. We entered into the whole experience with a great spirit of adventure. The following morning we were introduced to our fellow meditators and teachers. The atmosphere was tranquil and full of well-being—an all-embracing feeling of friendship and unity.

It was at lunchtime following a morning of peace, happiness and tranquillity, that we were forced brutally down to earth with a terrible bump. The courtyard of the college was buzzing with the sound of reporters. There was a very strange atmosphere in the air and it wasn't long before the bombshell hit us.

'I'm afraid we've got some very bad news for you lads,' said one very shocked looking reporter.

'What do you mean by bad news? What's happened? Come on give, will you? What's going on?' John asked, beginning to feel very worried.

'Well, fellers, I'm very sorry to have to break it to you this way but Brian is dead.'

A chorus of, 'But he can't be! We only saw him the other day. He was fine. There was nothing wrong with him. Christ, it just isn't possible, not Brian.'

It was quite a while before some had the presence of mind to ask how it had happened.

'Was it an accident? He wasn't ill, was he? How on earth did he die? He was so young.'

The outcome of all those fraught, shocked questions was a far from satisfactory answer. There was, however, some possibility that Brian had committed suicide. He had died of a drug overdose. He was alone in his country house and had only been discovered that morning after Peter Brown had failed to rouse him on the phone.

My feelings of impending doom were now an actuality. To describe our feelings as distraught would be putting it lightly. A great many tears were shed by our very unhappy group that morning. God and Christ must have been tired of hearing their names called, although they couldn't answer our repeated question, 'Why, why Brian?' We all felt at that moment that our world had been turned upside down. We just couldn't come to terms with the fact that we had lost our dear friend so tragically. It was all too much to comprehend, without trying to invoke an answer from the only God we knew.

At this point, when we didn't know where to turn, a messenger arrived from the Maharishi's quarters inviting us to join him. When eventually we pulled ourselves together, we entered the Maharishi's room. Maharishi was seated, lotus position, in the centre of a room filled to overflowing with flowers of every description and colour. The bright midday sun streamed through the casement windows filling the area with the most glorious iridescent colours. It was a most breathtaking sight, such a contrast from our grey depressed mood. The Maharishi embraced us all with his wisdom and understanding of our grief. His comforting words and enlightened reasoning slowly lifted us out of the depths of despair. He insisted that all the tears and sadness would not bring Brian back, but would in many ways hinder his journey. Our painful vibrations, he explained, would keep his spirit earthbound instead of free to rise to the next world. Brian, he said, would not want us to be unhappy but joyful. If we were joyful, therefore, Brian's spirit would find peace and joy. Like a relaxing balm, the Maharishi slowly brought us round to his way of reasoning. He even made us laugh. Anyone outside the room may have been very bewildered by the sounds of jollity. They may even have thought us callous in the light of the tragedy. But all I can say is that the Maharishi's words made our lives at that point full of hope and tranquillity. Our love for Brian was cemented by laughter not tears. We left Bangor in the early hours of the following morning. John and I sat in the back of the car stunned, yet calm. We both felt very strange, as though we were in a cocoon. There were no tears and no fears, just acceptance.

Brian's tragic, untimely death proved to be accidental. It was almost as though he had been put on this earth to do a job which was now finished. The Maharishi, it appeared, was to be our next teacher in life. And we welcomed his teachings and wisdom because we needed his guidance so much. Brian's death had thrown us to the

'Brian is dead long live Brian'

winds, yet the Maharishi was there to anchor us when we needed him most. The inevitable void at the loss was soon filled with plans for putting Brian's ideas into practice. A company called Apple Corps was formed. The Beatles' own recording label and the purchase of a property in Savile Row were fixed. A boutique in Baker Street was acquired. Four very way-out Dutch dress designers, who had befriended the Beatles, were given full rein as far as the designing of the clothes and painting of the shop was concerned. Hundreds of thousands of pounds were ploughed into their first business ventures, and before very long they had bitten off more than any of them could chew. Without Brian's stabilizing influence and innate business acumen the Beatles were totally vulnerable. The sharks, con-men and opportunists moved in with a vengeance. The Beatles' experience as far as business and high finance was concerned was nil. They were innocents in a very hard, cruel world stripped of all protection from themselves and the forces of evil.

The first disaster in business was the Apple Boutique. The building itself had been beautifully painted in psychedelic fashion by the Dutch designers. The opposition was incredible. The mass media went to town and so did the neighbouring shop owners. The painting would have to go. It was objectionable, disgusting and, above all, lowered the tone of Baker Street. The battle was fought and lost. The shop failed dismally to pay for itself, so the boys closed it down with a madness that befitted their state of mind at the time. The entire stock was given away.

The property in Savile Row cost a fortune to renovate and to install a recording studio. Luxurious furnishings and fittings were ordered and delivered. Drink cabinets were filled to overflowing. Every comfort was contained in that building, but the whole venture lacked a man such as Brian to take charge. It was like a ship without a captain and it sank lower and lower supporting the dead weight of numerous free loaders. It became a Mecca for drop-outs and out-of-work aspiring musicians. I could see us all being swallowed up in a quagmire of inefficiency. Big business was not their forte, and they had found themselves losing a game that they didn't know how to play.

It was with great happiness and lightness of heart that, following our initiation into the Maharishi's transcendental meditation centre, we discussed and planned a trip to India. It was time for us *all* to drop out for a while. The years of fame and fortune had taken their toll on our nerves and minds. The very thought of peace of mind and relief from pressure was so tempting. John and I both felt closer. There seemed to be a greater possibility of our finding a solution to personal difficulties. If our trip to India wasn't going to solve our emotional problems then nothing would. If meditation could rid us all of the rubbish and dross that we had been subconsciously absorbing over the past years, then perhaps we could start afresh with renewed strength of purpose and direction.

Our destination in India was to be the Maharishi's Meditation training centre in Rishikesh, high in the mountains on the banks of the fast flowing Ganges. It sounded like Shangri La to me, full of promise and hope. We were at the crossroads of life and fate it seemed might be pointing us in the right direction at last. We set off with great opitmism during the month of February 1968.

Our small party consisted of George, Patti, Jenny, Patti's younger sister, John and myself. Magic Alex also accompanied us. Paul, Jane, Ringo and Maureen had decided to join us at a later date. It was, after all, only John and George out of the four who really felt the need for the meditation. John and George found themselves at one when it came to discovering the mysteries of life. They were very sponge-like in their absorbence of new and fascinating dogmas. George's interest in the Sitar led him to become a very easy convert when it came to Indian philosophy. The Maharishi only fanned the already glowing embers of his curiosity. Previous to George's experiences with LSD and the subsequent flower power explosion, he had been the most tactless, blunt and often pig-headed of the four Beatles. George of course was the youngest and least mature, but to me he was the one Beatle who altered most in character and temperament over the years. He grew up very quickly, changing from a tactless youth into a sensitive, thinking individual. The rough edges were smoothed down and self-discipline became the cornerstone of his character. This was never more evident to me than in India.

Our arrival at Delhi airport went very much unheralded, apart from the odd local press representative. We were bundled unmolested and travel-weary into three battered, ancient Indian taxis without all of the usual fuss and frantic rush. It was wonderfully refreshing and stress free. We collapsed exhausted into the back seats of our allotted cabs surrounded by baggage enough to sink a battleship. Our journey took hours, but what a wonderful opportunity we had to observe the Indian way of life as we drove slowly through villages and towns teeming with turbaned, grinning characters. The colour and simplicity of life was truly fascinating. The market areas were alive with animals; oxen pulled broken-down carts urged on by local peasants. The motor car seemed to be totally out of place, time seemed to be standing still. The noise and excitement and atmosphere of the market place was all-enveloping. Indian delicacies were sizzling deliciously over numerous charcoal grills. The aromas of curry and sweetmeats made our mouths water. Children roamed the roads and side streets, almost naked but always smiling and waving. It was wonderful. What an experience!

The Maharishi's meditation centre eventually came into view as our long, tiring journey came to an end. Through an overgrown forest complete with elephants and tigers, we were driven to quite a high altitude. It was cold and wet, just coming to the end of the rainy season. The river Ganges crashed its way through the valleys and ravines below us, full and fast from the rains of the previous months. After alighting from the taxis, we were shown to our living quarters. The quarters consisted of a number of stone built bungalows, set in groups along a rough road. Flowers and shrubs surrounded them and were carefully tended by an Indian gardener whose work speed was dead slow, and stop.

Each buiding housed about five self-contained rooms with bathroom and two four-poster beds, one electric fire, a dressing table and chairs. It was spartan yet comfortable, above all peaceful. The Maharishi's dwelling was surprisingly modern and well equipped. It was surrounded by

168

beautiful blossoming plants and shrubs. A very well built lecture theatre was also part of the complex. It was the Maharishi's first training centre and I felt at the time that it was a very enterprising venture, by a very dedicated man.

Our fellow students had also arrived from various parts of the world. Actors, artists, teachers, businessmen and women, all lovely people bent on a vision of becoming better equipped to cope with life through transcendental meditation. Differing ages made little difference to the very close relationships and friendships which evolved during our stay in Rishikesh. It was only a short time before we all settled into the very happy and tranquil routines of meditation and lectures.

The days spent in Rishikesh began early. We woke between seven and eight o'clock; washed in freezing cold water (due to the fact that the plumbing left a great deal to be desired); breakfast was eaten out of doors about a hundred yards away from our billet. We would sit at a long table covered with plastic tablecloths held down by jars of jam and bowls of fruit. Young Indian boys fed us with masses of toast, coffee and tea. We were frequently joined for breakfast by an odd monkey or two which we would have to stop from whipping the very toast from our mouths. To eat communally overlooking the Ganges was a far cry from bacon and eggs in Surrey. A wooden trellis canopy over the dining area, entwined with creeping plants, sheltered us a little from the elements during these first weeks of cold and rain. Although our diet in India contained no meat or eggs, none of us suffered in any way. The luxuries we had grown used to became a dim and distant memory. We began to realize that we needed very little to find contentment. Instead of thinking about what next to buy to keep us happy, we thought more of what we didn't need. The simple life suited us all. We thrived and began to evolve more as individuals without stress and pressure.

As one day merged into the next, the weather altered dramatically. The sun shone and the heat created a marvellous feeling of well-being. Meditation and its effects began to show on us all. The Maharishi was a wonderful

teacher. His lectures and talks were humorous and enlightening and provided truly halcyon days. John and George
were in their element. They threw themselves totally into
the Maharishi's teachings, were happy, relaxed and above
all had found a peace of mind that had been denied them
for so long.

Meditation is a very solitary exercise and to partake one
has to be alone. John and I shared our room but found it
increasingly difficult to co-ordinate our timing as far as
meditation was concerned. For two people to meditate for
days on end in the confines of a single room was very dis-
turbing and difficult. The ideal situation we found was to
have our own separate rooms and do our own thing. I
think it was at this particular point that John and I began
really to go our separate ways, not necessarily mentally but
physically. Sometimes we met at mealtimes; sometimes not
at all. Depending on our meditation times, we would pass
each other on the winding paths between the different
buildings, wave, and pass the time of day. But the close-
ness that we felt at the time of Brian's death was slowly
disappearing. We were separate entities and contact was
infrequent.

Everything seemed to fall in place for me in India. I began to feel as though I was my own woman for the first
time. I depended on no one, spent hours drawing and
painting, chatting with fellow student teachers. In fact
John's complete involvement at first left me no other
choice. In fact, although I believe meditation is a wonderful exercise for mind and body, it was not for me the 'be
all and end all' of everything. To John nothing else mattered. He spent literally days in deep meditation, whereas
I would meditate intermittently and created, at other times,
designs and drawings for whoever wanted to hang them
on their walls. I loved the atmosphere in Rishikesh. Birth-
days were celebrated with fireworks; garlands made by
hand were hung around the neck of the lucky birthday
boy or girl. A celebratory party would follow, minus drink
of course.

I believed then and I believe now that the Maharishi is
a very wise and beautiful being. The press of the world
took great delight in trying to belittle him, their judgement

of him was not founded on experience of his teachings. No matter what anyone says about the Maharishi, he has always worked for the betterment of mankind. And if one man can even partially succeed in a single lifetime, then as far as I'm concerned he is worthy of praise not degradation or insult.

Just one of the Maharishi's acts of kindness was experienced by John and myself when we mentioned that it was our son Julian's birthday in the near future. Before we had time to turn around we were summoned to his quarters. On entering his rooms we were confronted by the Maharishi beaming with happiness when he saw our expressions of delight at what we saw. For Julian he had had the most beautiful Indian clothes made. They were fit for a little Indian prince, a complete wardrobe. Accompanying the clothes and set out on the floor around him was a complete set of exquisitely hand-painted figures of animals and authentic Indian hunters, John and I were overwhelmed. The Maharishi's kindness and thoughtfulness bowled us over. It was particularly unexpected in the stringent circumstances to which we had become accustomed in Rishikesh. On leaving the Maharishi, John held my hand. He was overjoyed.

'Oh, Cyn,' he said, 'won't it be wonderful to be together with Julian again. Everything will be fantastic again, won't it? I can't wait, Cyn, can you?'

I found it hard to believe that I was hearing John speak from the heart about our family for the first time in what seemed like years. It filled me with love and hope for our future.

Studying meditation and how to teach the subject made us all feel at times the way one does at school. Too much work and not enough play. We needed to let off steam. With the arrival of Paul, Jane, Ringo and Maureen, we relaxed a little on the study and spent afternoons sunbathing on the banks of the Ganges. Mia Farrow arrived and created a great deal of interest. Mike Love of the Beach Boys and Donovan also arrived with Gypsy his close friend. The interest and fascination with transcendental meditation was growing. Our very happy group seemed to be expanding by the minute. Patti and George were very happy in learning the sitar. John wrote some of his most beautiful lyrics and music dedicated to his mother, Julia. Donovan composed *Jennifer Juniper* for Patti's sister Jenny. I don't think I had ever before felt a stronger unity of happiness, contentment and creativity.

Unfortunately Maureen and Ringo stayed only for a short time, Maureen just couldn't stand the flies and insects, or the food. Ringo's stomach was weak from many operations as a child. Paul and Jane stayed longer but I felt that because they had missed the early stages of the course, and the growing feelings of friendship that we had all gained, they were very much on the fringe of activities.

Letting off steam entailed smoking, playing cards and on one occasion drinking. Drinking alcohol was strictly forbidden in Rishikesh. It was against all the principles of meditation and the Maharishi's teachings. But being human and a little rebellious, a bottle of Indian wine was smuggled into our quarters. God only knows how we got it past our lips. If we had put a naked flame to it, I'm sure it would have exploded. Nevertheless we all had a swig, shrieked, groaned and giggled at our madness. It was only a few days later that we were informed that a newspaper had printed an article about a sale of Indian alcohol which had poisoned hundreds of Indians in our area. That was the last time we indulged in Indian alcohol. Luckily none of us were sick, only sick with ourselves due to our lack of self-discipline. John and George did not imbibe. They did not feel the need to let off steam, only Patti, myself, Alexis and two American meditators. Alexis smuggled it in.

Excursions were planned by Maharishi in order that we didn't become too cut off from everyday life. The market town of Deradoon was our destination on one such an occasion. Wandering through the crowded bustling stalls which sold almost everything (saris of every describable colour, Indian jewellery, exquisite in its artistry and craftsmanship) poverty glared at us from behind outstretched hands. Crippled and deformed children tore at our clothes, begged for our support. Destitution and wealth on every corner. Gurus painted from head to toe with natural dyes sat motionless and cross-legged on the roadside, dead to the world and trying to attain their own nirvana. Incred-

172

ible sights, sounds and smells of India that we experienced at first hand, including shrines and temples so beautifully coloured, patterned and designed, so unlike our own grey stone solemn places of worship.

During our stay in Rishikesh, the Maharishi had taken the annual photograph of himself, his disciples and his students. This particular photograph created a great deal of excitement amongst the women of the group. We were all supplied with saris for the occasion (up until then we had been wearing very simple clothes made up for us by our own personal Indian tailors). The photograph of the group was taken in the overpowering heat of the afternoon sun, following a morning of learning how to wrap our saris. I must admit we all looked beautiful when finally we had sorted ourselves out. Our hair was put up and entwined with fresh flowers. Around our necks were hung garlands, also of fresh flowers. We were a sight to behold. The boys wore their Indian style western garb and looked equally impressive. It was quite an occasion, but by the time the session had come to an end our beautiful flowers had wilted; we had wilted; and sunburned bodies needed a great deal of soothing the following night. The Maharishi sat resplendent on his throne at the centre of his admiring followers. His laughter and good humour were ever present, laughter that rang out above everything like tinkling bells of joy. What a man!

We really wanted for nothing in Rishikesh, the Maharishi in his thoughtfulness would ask us all frequently if there was anything at all that we would like that he hadn't provided. He even arranged for an Indian lady masseuse to come for the girls. We all thought what a wonderful idea; how marvellous to have our very own masseuse. Little did we know how hilariously embarrassing the whole situation was to become. The lady was very sweet and obliging but the problem of communication was abysmal. At first, times were arranged for us to have our massage in our rooms. But the lady was so enthusiastic that she followed us around. To give you an example of how embarrassing the situation became, following a morning of meditation I would be relaxing and passing the time of day with a group of male and female meditators, when this little Indian lady would espy me from a great distance and hurry over smiling and talking to me very quickly in her own language. Under her arm would be all her oils and creams for massage. She would seat herself at my side and before I had chance to do anything or say anything she would grab hold of my arm or leg and with oil-filled hands proceed to massage vigorously. My attempts to put her off only created a more enthusiastic massage to my body. No matter what I did or said she would just nod and smile and pummel much to the amusement of my companions especially the males of the species. After a while we all learned that if we saw her coming it was the wisest course of action to turn on our heel and rush off in the opposite direction. Poor woman, she did mean well, and she was a marvellous masseuse, but . . . !

We spent blissfully happy days until yet another of those situations of acrimony arrived on our doorsteps. To me it was tragic—hearsay, an unproved action, and unproved statements. The finger of suspicion was well and truly pointed at the man who had given us all so much in so many ways—the Maharishi. Alexis and a fellow female meditator began to sow the seeds of doubt into very open minds. Meditation practised for long periods renders the meditator truly sensitive to any overt or strong vibrations. His mind becomes very finely tuned. Alexis's statements about how the Maharishi had been indiscreet with a certain lady, and what a blackguard he had turned out to be, gathered momentum. All, may I say, without a single shred of evidence or justification. It was obvious to me that Alexis wanted out and more than anything he wanted the Beatles out as well. The state of mind that George and John were in threw them into utter confusion. It really was too much for them to comprehend under the circumstances. A night was spent trying desperately to sort everything out in their minds, what to believe—Alexis' and this girl's accusation, or faith in the Maharishi. Indeed, a fellow meditator was particularly distrustful of Alexis. He said that he had seen Alexis in this girl's room, poring over a candle with her, and he believed that Alexis's influence over her was unhealthy. He believed that strange things were going on (and I did too; nothing seemed to ring

174

'It's very kind of you, but not today thank you!'

true). That night of soul searching by John and George produced a victory for Alexis and great unhappiness as far as I was concerned. Out of confusion and accusation came anger and aggression. Doubt and subterfuge replaced joy and peace of mind. The atmosphere was electric. An unreal situation was once more enveloping us and taking us over. It was a powerful situation that could not be fought. It seemed inevitable in its speed and directness of purpose. The Maharishi had been accused and sentenced before he had even had a chance to defend himself. All the bad thoughts were flowing back. Lack of faith and trust abounded, and the following morning, almost before any of us had a chance to wake up, Alexis set the ball in motion by ordering taxis to take us to the airport. That was how quickly things got out of hand, with the speed of an arrow.

The Maharishi must have been truly saddened when confronted by John and George. Their arguments and accusations were not based on evidence. They were confused and bitter at what they had learned, and yet they still didn't give the Maharishi a chance to defend himself. All they could say when asked was:

'If you're as cosmically conscious as you claim then you should know why we are leaving.'

With that they left him and returned to the dining-area where we were all waiting.

I have never packed my belongings with a such a heavy heart. I felt that what we were doing was wrong, very, very wrong. To sit in judgement on a man who had given us nothing but happiness . . . The real turning of the knife came as we were about to take our leave. While we were seated around the dining-tables waiting for the taxis and conversing in whispers, nerve ends showing, the Maharishi emerged from his quarters and seated himself not a hundred yards from our agitated group of dissidents. One of his ardent followers walked across to us and asked us to please talk things over properly with the Maharishi. He said he was very sad and wanted desperately to put things right and to convince us that we should stay.

I wanted to cry. It was so sad. The Maharishi was sitting alone in a small shelter made of wood with a dried

176

grass roof. He looked very biblical and isolated in his faith. His strength was being taken away from him through unproven statements and there seemed to be no way in which he could appeal to basic humanity and reason. The boys were adamant. They had made their minds up, burned their boats and nothing the Maharishi could do or say would budge them. They stood up, filed past him and not a word was said. I will never forget the picture in my mind. It may sound melodramatic but it was a very vivid impression of a scene from the Bible re-enacted in the mountains of India, of Jesus being denied by his disciples. Not that in any way did I believe that the Maharishi was Jesus, but to me he was a man with a quest, a dream for a better world and here were we, a group of people who had the power to influence the youth of the world possibly squashing all the good work he had done. The only person who actually stood up to be counted was the Maharishi, only subsequently to be shunned.

The journey away from my personal Shangri-la was miserable. Although John wasn't as glum as I, he was worried. He wanted to get home and quick. Although he had gone through the motions of rejecting the Maharishi and all he stood for, he was very nervous about the situation he now found himself in.

'God, Cyn, I won't feel safe until we're back in England. I feel as though the Maharishi is going to get his own back in some way.'

It was ridiculous, almost as though they were being pursued by some terrible enemy who was going to destroy them. Strangely enough we did have quite a set-back on our journey to Delhi. The taxis, as I described earlier, would have been in no condition to pass our MOT test, so it was our luck to break down somewhere in the Indian countryside. Our taxi gave up the struggle and steamed to a halt, flat tyre and no spare. The driver didn't speak English and we didn't understand a word he said but it did dawn on us when he took off down the road that perhaps he was going to get help. We found ourselves parked on a grass verge in the pitch dark without food or drink or any means of light, not a sign of life anywhere. The other taxis had gone on ahead, unaware of our predicament. It wasn't very long before John and I started to get the jitters.

'John, what on earth are we going to do, where are we? We're absolutely stranded without a penny or a friend in a foreign land, and I'm sure we've seen the last of our driver.'

John's only solution to the situation was to stand on the edge of the road with his thumb up in the air frantically waving it backwards and forwards at the sound of any car approaching. We were about to give up all hope when a saloon car drew up beside us and two very educated Indian men inquired after our health. Were we relieved!

After a great deal of humming and haa-ing we opted for the lift. At least we wouldn't freeze to death and they seemed very amiable and keen to help. The driver of the saloon was a very fast driver. John and I clung onto the front seats like grim death. They could have been maniacs for all we knew. We started to get really worried. Our imagination ran riot and we panicked. We were about to ask them to let us out when one of them made it known that they were aware that John was a Beatle and that they would do all they could to help us get back to Delhi. At that point we put ourselves entirely in their hands and believe me they did us proud. At the nearest village they bought us drinks, and arranged after a great deal of persuasion for another taxi to take us on the remainder of our long journey. Theye were really marvellous. They also arranged for our luggage to follow us on. When I look back I think we must have had a guardian angel looking over us.

Our eventual arrival at the hotel was even more chaotic. The driver took us on a tour of Delhi in order that we might remember where the hotel was. Finally the penny dropped, and the name came to us. We arrived about three hours later than everyone else and the consternation on their faces convinced us that they had all believed that we had been 'got'. Nevertheless, it was a warm, relieved reunion, full of questions and laughter at our story of disaster.

The idea was to try and book onto the first available

flight to England the next day, but as it happened Alexis discovered that we could just make a night flight which was due to take off within the hour. Once more I felt protest rise up inside me. I just couldn't understand why the mad rush. To me it was absolutely ridiculous; but a majority decision was made in favour of yet another speedy exodus.

During our flight I had a conversation with John about seven year itches. I don't know why I mentioned the subject, but I do remember John's impatient reply.

'Cyn, of course people feel the need to experiment. Do you know something, Cyn, you are really naïve!'

I must admit I was terribly naïve as far as John was concerned. I think I must have had a mental block. I never dreamed that he had been unfaithful to me during our married life. He hadn't revealed anything to me. I knew of course that touring abroad and being surrounded by all the temptations any man could possibly want would have been impossible to resist. But even so, my mind just couldn't and wouldn't accept the inevitable. I had never had anything concrete to go on, nothing tell-tale.

Discretion must have been John's middle name. During our marriage the only time that he gave me grounds for jealousy was at a private party and showing of *A Magical Mystery Tour*—the disastrous television film that the boys wrote and produced themselves following Brian's death and the Apple ventures.

The party was fancy dress and to be attended by numerous famous and infamous pop celebrities. It was a wonderful night. We all enjoyed the frivolity of dressing-up and making silly fools of ourselves. John really went to town. He went back in time and arrived as the greasiest and most objectionable looking Teddy boy, covered in chains and leather. I couldn't have been more opposite in my choice of dress. I looked like the lady on the front of a Quality Street tin, all crinoline, bonnets and bows. The party was progressing beautifully and when the dancing began it was take-your-partners-time. John made a bee-line for Patti who was looking incredibly sexy in her eastern-dancer's-seven-veils-and-not-much-else outfit. John hogged Patti for quite a time and I was left sitting primly and stiffly, very much out in the cold. A guest on our table, the lovely Lulu, also noticed John's over-enthusiastic attentions towards Patti, and sat next to me full of indignation at my plight. She really was funny, dressed in a Shirley Temple outfit of short spotted dress. Her hair was beautifully ringleted and tied at the top with a enormous bow, short white socks and a giant lollipop which finished off her detailed ensemble. Pint-sized Lulu took it into her head to give John a good telling off. It was such a lovely sight, Lulu cornering John and giving him what for. John was very much taken aback by Shirley Temple's serious lecture on how to treat his wife.

I wasn't totally without dancing partners, however. Billy J. Kramer was dressed as the *soldier* from Quality Street, and we made a lovely couple, until we tried to jive instead of waltz. Full of food and wine and high spirits I forgot my crinoline was not the right kind of dress for energetic gyrations and ended up red-faced on the floor, bonnet over my eyes and masses of material billowing out like a huge lavender balloon around my crumpled body. I always find that when I am trying to compete or make an impression I end up making a fool of myself. John's looks in my direction on that occasion were not of love or admiration, but pure embarrassment. I was letting him down yet again.

Voices flit like shadows down the passage of my mind.
They grow and fade in volume as the passing of the
    days
Bring memories of sunshine's timeless rays.
Times of childhood beckon calling me through days
    and years
Of happiness and loneliness mingled with the tears.

11

Yoko Ono

Although John said very little about the impression I made as his wife I always felt that he expected a great deal more of me. I really wasn't on his wavelength as much as he would have liked. He needed more encouragement and support for his way-out ideas. It wasn't very long after our return from India that I was to learn about how much John's need for a compatible companion was coming to the surface. Unbeknownst to myself or anyone else at the time John had been corresponding with a Japanese artiste and film-maker of way-out repute. The first time that I ever came in contact with Yoko Ono was at a meditation session in London. Prior to that, letters addressed to John had arrived at our home asking for his help and support in getting her book *Grapefruit* off the ground. She claimed that no one understood her work and that if someone didn't help her, she would give up everything. I had also been informed by Dot, the housekeeper, that she had been to the house on numerous occasions asking after John, but had been unlucky on all her visits.

I didn't think anything of this lady until the night of the meeting when she arrived all in black and sat quietly in the corner of the room. Something clicked inside my brain and I felt as though I was being threatened. Nothing was said. In fact it was all very innocent.

When I first met John his love was Brigitte Bardot but running a close second was the French Existentialist actress singer Juliet Greco. When I first set eyes on Yoko I knew that she was the one for John. It was pure instinct; the

181

chemistry was right; the mental aura that surrounded them was almost identical. I'm sure that at this point John had not even given it a second thought because when Yoko got into the car with us, as we were leaving to go home, John and I looked sideways at each other wondering what we were supposed to do with her. It was all very strange. Stranger still was a situation that arose following a weekend John spent away from home with a close business friend, who had a house in the country. He and his wife had numerous children and the atmosphere was usually chaotic, friendly and very homely. John returned over the moon. He was so happy and excited by what he had experienced. John had taken acid once more, but this time he said it was wonderful. His friend had told him that all was marvellous and that he was a great guy. This for John was such a revelation since he was always the one to boost others' egos. His own had been neglected until that moment.

'Cyn, it was great,' he enthused. 'Christ, Cyn, we've got to have lots more children. We've got to have a big family around us.'

At this point I burst into tears, much to John's amazement.

'What the hell's the matter with you, Cyn, what are you crying for?'

All I could blurt out was that in no way could I see us as he did. One trip did not guarantee a secure future and it was no use using the promise of a large family to solve our problems. I was so disturbed by John's outburst that I even suggested that Yoko Ono was the woman for him. John protested at my crazy suggestion and said that I was being ridiculous. But nothing he said could dissuade me from my premonitions.

Although life went on as usual, my fears grew. I felt nervous, depressed, as though I was sitting on the edge of a volcano. John was aware of my depression and suggested that as he had to work for long hours in the recording studios for a few weeks, I should accompany Jenny, Donovan, Gypsy and Alexis on a holiday to Greece. The very thought of sun and sea really brightened my outlook. I felt that the complete change would help me to get things

182

into perspective. I would be able to return refreshed and renewed. I felt that when I returned I would be able to cope with a situation that was fast getting out of hand.

The two weeks in Greece were wonderful, a total change. My mind began to unwind, the cobwebs of doubt and fear eventually began to disperse. I was happy and hopeful for the future. I had decided to banish my fears and premonitions. I wanted to be back with John again and to start afresh. All I could think of on the journey home was John and Julian and our future. We spent a night in Rome and following lunch the next day, we caught a flight back to London. I kept saying, 'Won't it be great! Lunch in Rome and we'll drag John out for dinner in London. We'll make a day of it, do the jet-set bit.'

Our arrival home, it seemed, was unexpected. It was four o'clock in the afternoon. The porch light was on and the curtains were still drawn. There were no signs of life, no Julian to welcome me with his usual shouts of delight, no John, no Dot, just an ominous silence. My heart was in my mouth. The front door was not locked so we all trooped into the house shouting, 'Hello, where are you? Is anyone home?' No response, until we walked into the morning-room where we heard quiet murmurings of conversation. When I opened the door I was confronted by a scene that took my breath and voice away. Dirty breakfast dishes were cluttering the table, the curtains were closed and the room was dimly lit. Facing me was John sitting relaxed in his dressing-gown. With her back to me, and equally as relaxed and at home, was Yoko.

The only response I received was 'Oh, hi,' from both parties. Although I knew that Yoko would in some way loom large in John's life, the reality and the shock of the situation stunned me more than I could have imagined. They looked so right together, so naturally self-composed under the unusual circumstances. I felt totally superfluous. The ground was taken from beneath my feet and I was incapable of dealing with such an occasion. I was a stranger in my own home. Desperately trying to cover up my shock, all I could think of saying was, 'We were all thinking of going out to dinner tonight. We had lunch in Rome and we thought it would be lovely to have dinner in London.

Are you coming?' It sounded so stupid in the light of the changed circumstances. The only reply I received was 'No thanks.' And that was it. I wanted to disappear and in fact that is just what I did. I rushed out of the room upstairs, gathered random personal belongings together with the speed of lightning. All I knew was that I had to get out, get away from a scene that created so much pain. I was in a terrible state of shock. As I ran along the landing, I noticed a pair of Japanese slippers neatly placed outside the guest bedroom door. Instead of feeling incensed, I just wanted to run. Jenny and Alexis were equally as shocked and embarrassed by the situation, so when I asked if I could stay with them for a few days they agreed readily.

Jenny and Alexis shared a small town house together in London. They did not live together as lovers, but as friends, and my arrival on the scene did not put them out in any way. They made me feel very welcome. I was really in a very bad way mentally at that stage. I had found a retreat for a while, but I didn't know what to do. I knew Julian was being cared for by Dot, but I ached to be with him. I just didn't know where to turn next, so I stayed for two or three days with Jenny and Alexis until the shock had subsided a little, and the reality of the situation had really dawned on me. I just had to face up to the truth and force a showdown by making my presence felt at home.

John and I sat down together to talk rationally about ourselves and our marriage. It evolved into a confessional. We poured out our true feelings for one another. John enlightened me about his infidelities and his fantasies involving other women and I listened once more hopeful for our future. At last we were getting down to the nitty gritty. It was a great outpouring of our failings and faults. When we had got it out of our systems, we were in tune once more. I felt very close to John and he put his arms around me, relieved of his guilt, and claimed that his love for me at that moment was stronger than it had ever been.

For a while everything was wonderful. We could speak more openly and honestly with each other and there really

184

was a glimmer of light at the end of the tunnel. John during this time was making arrangements with Paul to take a business trip to New York and as the time grew closer for him to go I pleaded with him to take me along. When he replied in the negative, I realized that that was it. John became withdrawn, irritable and nervous. I suggested that if I couldn't accompany him to America then I would like to take my mother and Julian back to Italy for a holiday. I didn't want to stay at home alone. I wanted the time away from him to go quickly. John did not try and dissuade me. He just acquiesced and drew more into himself.

The day of our departure arrived and my mother, noticing the change in John and his lack of enthusiasm for anything, tried desperately to bring him out of himself by suggesting that instead of her going to Italy, John should go instead.

When we left the house John did not even come downstairs to wave goodbye.

Once back in Italy, firmly ensconced in another of the Bassanini's hotels, I set about trying to give Julian and my mother a happy holiday. I pushed my worries to the back of my mind and behaved like Nero as Rome burned —only I couldn't fiddle. I just lived from day to day without even contemplating the future. My aunt and uncle also joined us on our holiday, so I was secure in the bosom of my family, as it were. Whilst staying in the Hotel Cruiser I was introduced to Signore and Signora Bassanini's son Roberto, who spoke English. He assisted his mother, at her request, to communicate with me. Roberto was friendly and open, always entertaining his cronies in the hotel bar. It was during the second week of my holiday that I struck up a friendship with a Lancashire girl who worked as a waitress at the hotel. She was full of fun and energy and had obviously been observing the quiet uneventful holiday I had been having. She suggested that I went out on the town with her to see a bit of the night life. The night that she made her suggestion found me feeling rather weak, and sickening for laryngitis. I was low and depressed. My response at first was negative, explaining that we would be fair game with all the bottom-pinch-

185

ing Italians if we ventured anywhere without an escort, and I definitely wasn't looking for that sort of night out. The confident Lancashire lass shouted me down by saying that Roberto would take us out. He's always out on the town, and he's lots of fun. So with that sorted out, we conned Roberto into being our escort for the night. Much to the delight of my mother and relations, who were very worried about my state of mind, they encouraged me to go.

'Go on, love, go and enjoy yourself; don't worry about Julian. I'll look after him. Anyway you look as though you need a bit of fun,' urged my mother.

On our return in the early hours of the morning, who should be standing outside on the pavement but a very agitated Alexis. It must have appeared to him on that fateful night that I was having a wonderful illicit holiday romance. His face dropped when he saw me. My mother was sitting in the hotel lobby looking very upset and worried. Alexis was carrying an ultimatum, and that ultimatum was for me, a messenger bearing ill tidings. When I asked him what was the matter, his reply rushed out and rooted me to the ground. I was tired, ill, my strength drained away from me as he said,

'John is going to divorce you and take Julian away from you. He has sent me to tell you.'

'He is going to take Julian off you and send you back to Liverpool.'

The moment that I had feared most was upon me, but all I could think was how cruel and cowardly was the act. But knowing John as well as I did, it didn't really surprise me. His unprincipled behaviour and actions were born out of panic. It was easier and less painful for him this way. With me thousands of miles away, he could block his mind to the seriousness of his actions and lose himself in his newfound love.

All the worry and confusion he had experienced before my departure had culminated in the ultimate decision of breaking up our marriage. I understood his fears and misgivings, his actions were in keeping with his character, instant and immovable. John had made his mind up, burned his boats, and wanted it over as quickly as possible. He had to be himself regardless.

186

Whilst I was away Yoko moved in, revealing to the world their intentions. John had at last found his soul-mate and I had been aware of it even before he had. Alexis returned to England and I took to my bed. I was very ill both in mind and body. The hotel doctor insisted that I stay in bed until I was strong enough to travel, a journey that I did not relish. My whole world was collapsing in ruins around me and I had to find the inner strength from somewhere to face what would inevitably be a dreadful uproar of publicity and legal wrangles. My mother was a great tower of strength. She insisted that I stay in bed until I was well enough to face the furore, while she returned to England to see at first hand what the situation was. I was too weak to argue. My aunt and uncle cared for Julian and my mother left with a very heavy heart. It was such a terrible experience. I was totally helpless to do anything and kept thinking that I would wake up and everything would be back to normal. But no, my mind took flight and drifted in circles somewhere above my body. I knew it was true, but accepting the facts as they had been put to me, crippled my senses and reasoning powers. I was floating and my feet were not touching the ground any more.

I didn't blame John or Yoko. I understood their love. I knew I couldn't fight the unity of mind and body that they had with each other. I had after all subconsciously prepared myself for what had happened. But the implementation of their love for each other was without feeling for anyone else at the time. Their all-consuming love had no time for pain or unhappiness. That was to be dismissed as speedily as possible, just as quickly as the Maharishi had been dismissed and dispensed with. I was to be dealt the selfsame blow. Yoko did not take John away from me, because he had never been mine. He had always been his own man and had always done his own thing, as I had learned to do because of my life with him. I had grown to be independent of John; the testing time I went through on my return home proved that to me. I was shocked, shattered and lost, but not weak. The moment Julian and I arrived back in England we were driven straight to my

187

mother's flat in the centre of London. There was nowhere else for me to go. Within an hour of my arriving, there was a knock on the door. My mother opened it and was promptly handed a sealed official looking envelope to be given to me. When I opened it I really couldn't believe my eyes. The contents revealed a divorce petition accusing *me* of adultery. Well, that really took the biscuit. I found it hard not to admire John's style, the best form of defence is attack. But I couldn't believe that it was happening to me. I hadn't even had a chance to discuss anything with John. I was being cut off like a gangrenous limb with the speed of a surgeon's scalpel. My first thoughts were to obtain an audience with my husband. To do this I had to make an appointment through Peter Brown at the Apple offices. Peter was very sheepish about the whole crazy situation, but said that he would do what he could. Because I had no one on my side, as it were, my mother sent a telegram to my eldest brother who was working and living in Libya at the time. He took the first flight home to assist me in finding a reputable lawyer. We rushed around like mad things trying to find a solution to my dilemma. Eventually we were successful in finding someone to act for me.

A meeting was arranged between myself, John and Yoko at our home in Weybridge. It was nerve-wracking and highly charged emotionally, but fruitless as far as common sense was concerned, an absolute waste of time and nervous energy. John's accusations of my infidelity fell very much on stony ground and led me to petition him for divorce within the day.

Julian and I moved back into our home with my mother. John and Yoko moved into my mother's flat, which was one of Ringo's assets and we tried desperately to pick up the pieces once more.

John had shattered the equilibrium of the tightly knit Beatles family. His actions had stunned and confused everyone. But it was obvious that they could do without a Cynthia, but not without their leader.

During the divorce proceedings I was truly surprised when one sunny afternoon Paul arrived on his own. I was touched by his obvious concern for our welfare and even more moved when he presented me with a single red rose accompanied by a jokey remark about our future, 'How about it, Cyn. How about you and me getting married?'

Paul's request was purely jocular and designed to lift my spirits. We both laughed at the thought of the world's reaction to an announcement like that being let loose. On his journey down to visit Julian and I Paul composed the beautiful song *Hey Jude*—he said it was for Julian. I will never forget Paul's gesture of care and concern in coming to see us. It made me feel important and loved, as opposed to feeling discarded and obsolete. Paul gave me a great deal of strength and hope, and I thank him for it.

There were many sacrifices during the heady, frenzied Beatle years. Stuart, Brian, many were hurt, used and discarded. You had to be strong to keep up with the madness and unreality. Although I was the first to go before they finally disintegrated, I can only thank God for giving me enough inner strength to survive and overcome the shock and disappointments in a marriage which was to say the least 'very interesting'. I experienced a life and life-style which must have been envied by millions. I met people whom I admired and loved and people who shocked and disgusted me. I learned how the other half lived, and how many died in pursuit of an instant understanding of life and its meaning. I can only sum up my story by appealing to people's understanding when judging the actions, feelings, successes and inevitable mistakes which were made by four very young men, who, at an age when they would have been learning how to cope with life and learning a trade, found themselves with the world at their feet. To me it is in their favour that they are still sane and coherent. I still feel very proud of the Beatles and their accomplishments. My life during that period was an education, an education I wouldn't have missed. It has left me feeling enriched, not embittered, enlightened not blinded. All I can think of to conclude my story is to say, 'Thanks for the memories, and in the words of the I CHING, no blame.'

189

Raindrops

My love is on the wind this day
It flies through space and emptiness.
Carrying raindrops, tears of love,
Caressing waves of tenderness.
Thoughts fall in pools of sadness
On the pillow of my dreams.
My heart is like the wilting flower
Tossed by wind and rain.
Struggling both to tower above the storm again.

SNOW BLIND

ROBERT SABBAG

A BRIEF CAREER IN THE COCAINE TRADE

From Amagansett to Bogotá, from straight to scam to snafu then the slam, SNOWBLIND is an all-out, nonstop, mind-jolting journey through the chic and violent world of Zachary Swan, the real-life Madison Avenue executive who embarked on a fabulous, shortlived career in smuggling—bringing better living through chemistry from South American soil to New York nose.

 AVON/44008/$2.50